NEWMAN: A SHORT BIOGRAPHY

MICHAEL COLLINS

Published by Messenger Publications, 2019

ISBN 978 1 78812 105 7

Designed by Messenger Publications Design Department
Ornate letters by Song Mi / Shutterstock
William Morris background design / Shutterstock
Typeset in Sabon LT Pro and Pompei Pro
Printed by Hussar Books

Messenger Publications,
37 Lower Leeson Street, Dublin D02 W938
www.messenger.ie

CONTENTS

Introduction 7

Chapter 1: Setting the Scene 11

Chapter 2: Oxford 19

Chapter 3: Vicar at St Mary's 35

Chapter 4: Conversion to Catholicism 47

Chapter 5: Becoming a Catholic Priest 55

Chapter 6: The Oratory 63

Chapter 7: The Catholic University 69

Chapter 8: Return to Birmingham 87

Chapter 9: Apologiae 95

Chapter 10: Cardinal Newman 107

Chapter 11: Newman's Last Years 119

Chapter 12: Saint in the Making 125

Epilogue 129

Appendix 133

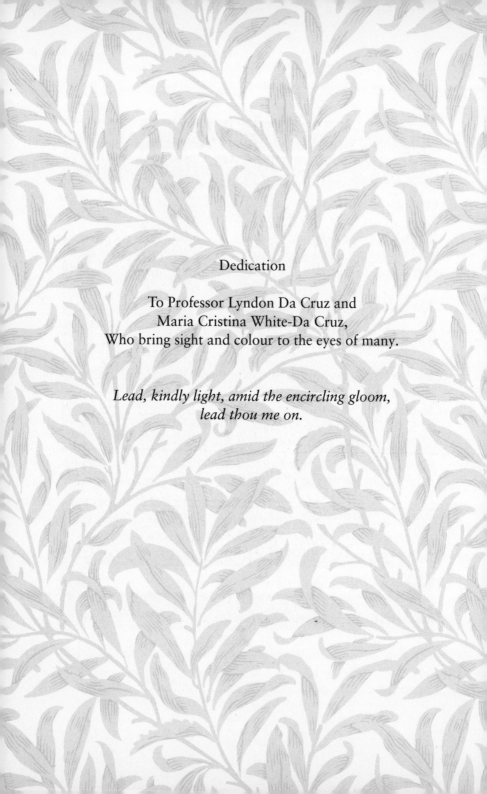

Dedication

To Professor Lyndon Da Cruz and
Maria Cristina White-Da Cruz,
Who bring sight and colour to the eyes of many.

*Lead, kindly light, amid the encircling gloom,
lead thou me on.*

John H. Card. Newman.

'*The best place to find John Henry Newman is at his desk.*'
Photograph of Newman taken 1861.

INTRODUCTION

The best place to find John Henry Newman is at his desk. For most of his life he read, studied and poured out his thoughts on paper. Sometimes these thoughts became letters to family and friends, other times allocutions or sermons, and yet other times became books that exerted significant influence on his contemporaries.

As a young man he stood while writing, books balanced on a mahogany desk as he worked on his text. He collected and read thousands of books in English, Latin and Greek. For some eight decades he carried on a vast correspondence with people at home and abroad. Over the course of his eighty-nine years, he penned a vast array of writings, thousands of letters, books, novels, diaries and even two autobiographical works, which were crafted carefully for his audience.

Newman was dismissive of biographies. 'A man's life is in his letters,' he wrote to his sister Jemima in 1863. 'I sincerely wish to seem no better nor worse than I am.' In the last years of his life, the diminutive black-robed figure spent much of the day in his book-lined study, putting his letters in order. They do contain his soul. There are close on 20,000 surviving letters – to date, thirty volumes have been published. In some letters Newman cajoles, in some he complains, while in others he encourages his reader. His first letters were to family and close friends, but by the end of his life he had a vast network of both professional and personal acquaintances.

Newman's voice becomes clearer as one reads his letters. He complains of fatigue, or worries scrupulously about small matters. He is often overly sensitive. He seeks to be gentle but his words can also be harsh, cutting like a razor. He is a conflicted soul, rarely writing succinctly, but setting out two sides of every argument before seeking out the middle ground.

To the modern reader, Newman's writings appear dated and his style is not easy to grasp. Only occasionally does he paint a scene for the reader to imagine. He is more interested in getting his views across. The Victorians were prolific letter writers for, apart from speech, there was no other way to communicate. Today Newman would undoubtedly have his own newspaper column and blog. He would struggle to limit himself to social media posts of 280 characters.

Our world is undoubtedly different from that of the Victorian era. So much has changed in the past century and a half, for good and evil. Newman's writings can still contribute to many areas, but part of his fascination lies in his complex character. He struggled in his personal and professional relationships and, above all, he developed an extraordinary and all-pervasive relationship with God. He wrote continuously on the horizon between heaven and earth, and for this reason he continues to draw the enquiring mind and the open heart.

Newman's desk in the Birmingham Oratory.

CHAPTER 1:
SETTING THE SCENE

ondon at the time of Newman's birth had expanded over the 1,750 years since its foundation by Roman settlers in AD 50. It became the capital of England in the twelfth century and continued to grow in importance, due in large part to the presence of the royal court. By 1800, the city numbered more than a million inhabitants. The nineteenth century witnessed an unprecedented boom as the British empire expanded, and by 1900 London was the largest city in the world with a population in excess of six million inhabitants.

As it grew, London became a city of contrasts. No other writer captured the sense of the city and its colourful characters better than Charles Dickens. London had magnificent public buildings and institutions, and miserable slums and poorhouses. As the gentry built elegant residences and employed domestic servants, migrants, especially the impoverished Irish, filled the city to fuel the burgeoning economy.

The banks of the Thames, the artery of commerce, housed the docklands, rife with prostitutes and a warren for murderers. The stench of the East End was infamous and few, beyond its inhabitants, ventured into the maze of streets where refuse and excrement harboured typhoid, dysentery and cholera.

The Industrial Revolution in England developed production methods that had not changed for centuries. The spinning jenny transformed the woollen industry, while the steam engine heralded the locomotive. Coal, used to fuel factories and heat homes, turned the buildings black with carbon deposits and poisoned the citizens. Trains, trams and omnibuses pushed people out to settle in new suburbs, covering acres of green land

and verdant forests with red and brown brick houses. While the rich strolled down the fashionable streets to visit their tailors or jewellers, the poor queued outside pawnbrokers, clutching their miserable possessions, which they lent the brokers until times improved. Often, rather than improving, they deteriorated, and the pubs and alehouses became the refuge of their wretched lives. When all hope died they were literally carted off to the workhouses or prison. Disease ensured that the last chapters of their lives were mercifully short, and every cemetery had a plot where paupers were thrown and covered with quicklime.

Nor was this phenomenon confined to London. Cities such as Manchester and Birmingham repeated the excesses of London. The rich accumulated wealth and occasionally salved their consciences by contributing to charities such as Thomas Coram's Foundling Hospital, or the almshouses administered by several parishes.

Men were encouraged to join the army, at once relieving national unemployment while simultaneously expanding the empire upon which, in the words of the hymn, the sun never set. Queen Victoria, whose reign began in 1837, and her consort, Prince Albert, sought to strengthen ties between the royal houses of Europe through marital alliances. The country was ruled by the monarch and governed by parliament without a constitution. Socially, divorce was prohibited by law, abortion confined to the back streets and visible homosexual acts were criminal and punishable with hard labour or exile. The death penalty was administered by hanging, and executions took place in public.

Christianity, in its various forms, was the predominant religion of Britain. St Augustine was sent by Pope Gregory the Great to bring the faith to the Angles in the late sixth century and, over the centuries, Christianity gradually spread across the land. Catholicism, with its loyalty to the pope, was banished in the mid-sixteenth century when Henry VIII established himself as head of the Church of England in an effort to provide a legitimate heir to the Tudor throne. The last great split within the Anglican Church came when the Methodists broke away at the end of the eighteenth century.

Successive monarchs granted privileges to the Anglican Church, while new movements, such as Methodism and Liberal Christianity, gained popular support. The Salvation Army, founded in 1865 by the Methodist preacher William Booth, offered practical help with food and clothing, thus alleviating poverty to some degree. In 1829, Catholic Emancipation ended almost two centuries of penal laws, leading to a gradual although uneven improvement of the position of Catholics in society. But even their assimilation was slow. Jews, who worked largely in banking, the legal profession and the clothes trade, were the largest non-Christian group in England.

Despite the gloomy excesses of the century, London expanded in power and finance. Several museums and national art galleries opened or expanded. The British Museum was founded in 1753 and the National Gallery in 1824. Great Britain emerged from the Napoleonic Wars greatly enhanced, and throughout the nineteenth century the nation was the most economically prosperous in Europe, dubbed 'the workshop of the world'. Despite the disparity of wealth, and the poverty of so many, Britain developed an almost impregnable belief in its superiority. The Victorian era was marked by strict social convention, and the Victorians themselves believed they were the most enlightened and civilised people to inhabit the British Isles.

John Henry Newman was born in London, at 80 Old Broad Street, on 21 February 1801. The house has long since been demolished, although a plaque commemorates the site. His parents, John Newman and Jemima Fourdrinier, had been married in 1799 at Lambeth in Surrey. Jemima, a descendant of prosperous French Huguenot papermakers and printers, was twenty-nine and her husband was thirty-four. John, whose immediate ancestors were from East Anglia and Holland, was a banker in the financial district of Lombard Street. His father was a grocer who had moved from Cambridgeshire to London. John founded a bank with his uncle and cousin, Richard and James Ramsbottom, which allowed him purchase a four-storey brick house in Southampton Street. It was a stone's throw from Bloomsbury Park in a settled, respectable area. John Henry was baptised on 9 April that same year by the Reverend Robert Wells at the parish church of St Benet Fink.

In later years Newman recalled his parents with great affection. He had a tender love for his mother who was devout and read him stories from the Bible. His father was typical of his age, talking little about his religious beliefs but nonetheless assiduous in the practice of his Anglican faith. Newman remembered his paternal grandmother and his father's sister with particular affection

The following year Jemima gave birth to a second son, Charles Robert. The first daughter, Harriet Elizabeth, was born in 1803, followed by a third son, Francis William, in June 1805. Jemima employed a nanny to assist her in caring for the four infants. A second daughter, Jemima Charlotte, was born in 1808, followed by Maria Sophia in 1809.

The middle-class family was able to provide early schooling at home with a governess, Mary Holmes, and in 1808, when Newman was seven, he was enrolled in Great Ealing School, which had been founded in 1698. Ealing was regarded as one of the finest schools and had a strong emphasis on sports, in which the boy had little interest. Louis Philippe, the future king of France, taught mathematics, a discipline in which Newman soon excelled. Directly across the road was the parish church of St Mary and the parish poorhouse.

Newman was a voracious reader, devouring exotic tales such as the Arabian Nights and the stories of Ulysses and Aeneas. While the boys played cricket, 'fives' tennis and other team games in the adjacent fields or swam in the school pool, Newman remained in the classrooms, neatly dressed in a waistcoat and trousers. His vivid imagination absorbed a vast amount of literature. One of the earliest surviving letters came from the then eight-year-old John Henry, written in beautiful copperplate to his mother.

Newman held the headmaster, Reverend Dr George Nicholas, then in his late thirties, in high regard. The school produced notable figures of the Victorian era, including the novelist William Thackeray, the biologist Thomas Huxley, the librettist William Schwenck Gilbert, the sculptor Richard Westmacott and Henry Rawlingson, a noted scholar of Assyrian cuneiform. Reverend Walter Mayers of Pembroke College, Oxford, was a regular visitor to the school and later John Henry was to attribute to him the means by which he came to a lively religious faith.

The school day was divided between lessons and physical exercise. Newman learned to dance, sing, fly kites and play cards and chess. He climbed trees and garnered a small group of like-minded friends who formed a secret society of which he was the leader. From time to time he won a book on prize-giving day. In addition to Latin, which he began to study at the age of nine (and Greek the following year), he added French, a language that was highly regarded at the time. At school he begin his studies in the viola, which was to be his companion until the last years of his life. He also had his first horse-riding lessons.

Newman boarded with some 290 other boys and, once a month, each child was able to go home on Saturday afternoon, returning on Sunday evening before supper. School holidays were valued by Newman chiefly because they afforded him time for uninterrupted reading. He recalled in latter life how he read the novels of Sir Walter Raleigh before it was time to get up and he also delighted in other novels, which he read throughout the day. He developed a precocious interest in religious literature. Writing in a brief autobiography five decades later, Newman recalled a French priest who taught English at school and a couple of Catholic families in the village. Apart from those isolated figures, the young man's world was entirely Anglican.

At the age of fifteen, a little over a year before he left school, the teenager had a religious experience which had a profound and lasting effect on his personality. Years later Newman described it as a conversion that made him more aware of the presence and majesty of God. It was a gradual realisation that matured between August and December 1816, and it was during these months that he decided to lead a celibate life according, as he believed, to God's will. He recounted this religious experience in his brief autobiography as being 'more certain than that I have hands or feet'. The religious awakening came about through reading works by the sixteenth-century Swiss reformer, John Calvin, and his followers. The young Newman was deeply impressed with this Evangelical Protestantism. It concentrated on the personal salvation of each individual, which had been obtained by Jesus' atonement with God the Father. Evangelical preachers underscored the grace by which each sinner had been saved by Jesus' death. This resonated with a form of piety the young boy had learned from his mother. He also read Joseph Milner's *Church History* and Newton's *The Prophecies*, which introduced him to the Catholic religion and convinced him that the pope was the antichrist.

On 8 March 1816 Newman's father's bank had collapsed due to the effects of the Napoleonic Wars and he was unexpectedly faced with the task of paying creditors and searching for new employment. The family were forced to move to Alton in Hampshire, where John senior secured employment managing a brewery.

Having graduated from school in early 1816, Newman had to consider his future career. His first thought, and at his father's prompting, was to enrol at Lincoln's Inn to study law, but he decided instead to study humanities at Trinity College, Oxford. Newman successfully sat an entrance exam for Trinity College, where he commenced a degree in Classics and mathematics on

14 December 1816. The following year, on 8 June, he came into residence within the college and on 30 November he made his Holy Communion in the collegiate chapel. Among his fellow students was George Spencer, son of Earl John Spencer, who subsequently converted to Catholicism and became a celebrated member of the Passionist Congregation.

Given his father's precarious financial situation and encouraged by his tutor Thomas Short, the young Newman sat for a scholarship on 18 May 1818. He was successful and was awarded tuition and sustenance fees.

CHAPTER 2:
OXFORD

Line engraving of Trinity College, Oxford, from Broad Street.

The twin universities of Oxford and Cambridge were the premier seats of learning in Victorian England. Monks studied at Oxford as early as 1096 and the university expanded in 1167 when Henry II banned English students from studying at the University of Paris. After a row between Oxford students and townsfolk in 1209, several students and tutors moved east to Cambridge where they founded a new college. With the break with Rome under King Henry VIII, both universities became Anglican and remained so until 1856.

Trinity College, Oxford, dated from 1555, when Thomas Pope bought Durham House where the monks of Durham Abbey and cathedral had studied since 1291. The house had been appropriated by Henry VIII in 1545. The elegant sandstone building was small, and there were no more than a few score undergraduates, who attended a number of tutorials each week.

Newman was impressed by the work of a former fellow of Trinity, Thomas Newton, who later became Bishop of Bristol and Dean of St Paul's in London, and by the Cambridge-educated clergyman, Joseph Milner, and his brother Isaac, who wrote the *History of the Church of Christ*. Of all the works Newman read in his early years at Trinity, *A Commentary on the Whole Bible*, by Reverend Thomas Scott, made the deepest impression. Newman tried unsuccessfully to meet Scott, who was also one of the founders of the Church Missionary Society.

Oxford tuition consisted of reading widely according to texts prescribed by the tutor and discussing them in private sessions. Books were expensive and a large selection, many of them centuries old, was kept in the oak-panelled library. Books could be requested from the librarian who curated the volumes. Medieval manuscripts were still commonly available in college libraries in Newman's day. During term time, he studied for ten hours a day, and up to fourteen close to exams.

Students, usually no more than half a dozen, gathered in the rooms of their tutors weekly. The tutor discussed the reading material that had been set the previous week and answered questions. The students boarded in the college, attended Matins and Evensong in the college chapel and dined in Hall. Discipline was strict and undergraduates were expected to honour their college. Drunkenness or other forms of poor behaviour were admonished and punished.

The first written glimpse of John Newman's propensity for friendship occurred in November 1818 when, along with his new friend J.W. Bowden, he composed two cantos, entitled *St Bartholomew's Eve*. Newman showed delight at finding a friend who shared his passion for the romantic medieval world.

Newman also read the more secular works of the historian Edward Gibbon, whose *Decline and Fall of the Roman Empire* fascinated him, and the works of the Enlightenment philosopher David Hume. He diligently attended his tutorials with Dr Thomas Short, submitted written essays and was confident of achieving a good grade in his final examination. At his father's insistence, he put his name down for Lincoln's Inn in 1819, with the intention of studying law.

Shortly after his final examination for a Bachelor of Arts taken on 5 December 1820, the results were posted on the board opposite the porter's lodge inside the main arched entrance. Newman had been called for the examination a day before he expected. To his shock and bitter disappointment, he did poorly, achieving only a third-class BA degree. He smarted under the humiliation, but years later he claimed that his father's financial situation had prevented his studying for an honours degree.

On 1 November 1821 his father was declared bankrupt. Everything in the house was sold. When he was in extreme old age, a Mrs Fox wrote to Newman saying that she had come across old viola scores inscribed with his name.

While he hoped to remain at Oxford, there was little chance that he could find a position at Trinity College. He now had to make the difficult choice between applying to another college for a fellowship or returning to London in the hope of finding employment.

Becoming a fellow at an Oxford college required that one remain celibate and unmarried. It was a throwback to the era when monks were lecturers and taught their novices. Those who accepted fellowships knew the sacrifices that would be required for the needs of the college. Teaching was not a well-paid profession and fellows often became clergymen in order to have 'a living', or parish, which would supplement their income and provide a residence in later life. On 11 January 1820, John Henry had decided to take Holy Orders in the Church of England. Some weeks later, he applied to Oriel College in the hope of receiving a fellowship and thus becoming a member of the academic staff, for which lodgings were provided.

Oriel, Oxford's oldest college with a royal charter, had been founded under Edward II in 1326. The holdings of the library dated to the mid-twelfth century and the college had been largely rebuilt in the mid-seventeenth century. Although a small college, it was elegant and had a good reputation for theology, medicine and law, and boasted eminent graduates such as Henry VIII's chancellor, Sir Thomas More, adventurer and writer Sir Walter Raleigh and many members of the British aristocracy. The college's reputation had taken a downturn in the early eighteenth century, but between 1780 and 1830, the provost and fellows improved academic standards by extending the library and raising teaching qualifications.

Newman's brother Francis arrived in Oxford to study Classics in 1821 and they lodged together over Seal's Coffee Shop on Broad Street. Francis was just as committed a Christian as his brother and soon made his mark as a talented linguist.

23

Becoming a fellow at Oriel required reading for an oral exam on set material. Several of Newman's friends advised him not to put himself forward, but he was determined to try, and on 5 February 1822 he put his name on the list of candidates. He took digs in Oxford and taught a number of pupils to support himself. The young graduate was now developing an interest in the early Church Fathers, bishops and theologians primarily of the fourth and fifth centuries. Writing in Latin and Greek, authors such as Athanasius of Alexandria, Basil and Gregory of Cappadocia, Ambrose of Milan and Augustine of Hippo sought to expand the horizons of Christian theology as it took root in the Greco-Roman world.

On 12 April 1822 Newman was elected a fellow of Oriel College, having been chosen from ten candidates to fill one of two vacancies. Newman's proficiency in Latin and Greek, as well as his interest in patristics, the study of early Christian theology, ensured his success on the first attempt. Employing Newman improved the Oriel's offering of early Christian history. Some years later his niece Anne Mozley wrote that John Henry called it the 'turning point' in his life, and 'of all days most memorable'. When the porter's messenger came to tell Newman the news, he found him playing the viola.

His election as a fellow was a tremendous relief. Following tradition, he paid for the bells of Trinity College to toll his success and that evening he dined with his new colleagues, Hawkins, Keble, Tyler and other academics, in the fellows' common room.

The position was for life and assured Newman of a secure financial future. He was required to take an Oath of Submission to the Thirty-Nine Articles, the foundational document of the Anglican Church. Soon after his election he was appointed pro-proctor and assigned a velvet-stripped gown of office.

College life was congenial. A hearty fried breakfast with porridge and cream was offered each morning in Hall. The fellows' common room on the ground floor to the rear of the college had a long table where members could dine on excellent food and enjoy the well-stocked wine cellar. The newspapers were delivered each day to keep the academics informed. The chapel had a choir that provided music for services.

Newman now made his first foray into professional publishing. Richard Whately, a fellow of Oriel, knew that Newman could do with some extra income and asked him to assist him in working on *Dialogues of Logic*, which he had prepared for his students and now wanted to publish in book form. Whately also asked William Rowe Lyall, editor of the *Encyclopaedia Metropolitana*, to commission Newman to write some entries. The first instalment of the encyclopedia had been published in 1818, in part to counteract the secular *Encyclopaedia Britannica*, which had appeared in twenty volumes the previous year. Newman's contributions were on miracles, Cicero and Apollonius. He later expressed his gratitude to Whately for assisting his style of writing and also helping him overcome his shyness, although his politics differed from Whately's.

During these early years at Oriel, Newman formed another close lifelong friendship with Edward Bouverie Pusey, who had become a fellow in 1823.

Many fellows became clergymen. While they kept rooms at their college and taught there, they were able to work in parishes, sometimes availing of local lodgings. Shortly after he began as a fellow, John Henry began to prepare to become a clergyman.

Theological instruction was given during tutorials, and even informally on walks. From Dr William Jones Newman learned about apostolic succession, the concept that the episcopal office was handed down from bishop to bishop since the time of the twelve apostles. During the summer of 1823, Newman accompanied Dr Jones around Christchurch meadow while the academic spoke about the apostolic tradition. While the concept was not of great interest at the time, Jones's words remained with Newman for many years and he recalled how the biblical lands seemed to come alive along the banks of the River Ox.

As part of his theological training John Henry and the

other ordinands studied the Thirty-Nine Articles. These had been formulated over five decades and were printed in 1571 in the *Book of Common Prayer*. The articles, largely the work of Archbishop Thomas Crammer (+1556) and Archbishop Matthew Parker (+1575), both archbishops of Canterbury, set out the doctrines of the Anglican Church from Henry VIII to Elizabeth I.

Prior to ordination as priests, candidates are ordained deacons, serving for about a year. Accordingly, on 13 June 1824 John Henry Newman was ordained in Christchurch, a foundation dating from the reign of Henry VIII. Ten days later the Reverend Mr Newman delivered his first sermon as a deacon at nearby Holy Trinity Church, Over Worton, where Reverend Walter Mayers, who had taught Newman Classics at Greater Ealing School, was vicar. Newman's first text was 'Man goeth forth to his work and unto the evening'. Nineteen years later he would preach his last sermon as an Anglican clergyman on the same text.

In order to gain pastoral experience, new deacons were assigned to a parish for a short time. Newman was assigned to St Clement's, a rapidly expanding parish near Oxford. Between 1821 and 1825, 300 new houses were built in the parish area. The church seated only about 300 worshippers and the parish vestry undertook to build a new church nearby to accommodate the thousand new parishioners. The octogenarian rector, Reverend John Gutch, had no appetite either to fundraise or to work on the project.

On 4 July 1824 Newman began his pastoral work at St Clement's, although he retained his lodgings at Oriel College. Each day he walked to and from the parish. He worked assiduously to learn the names of as many parishioners as possible. With youthful enthusiasm he filled notebooks with the occupations of each parishioner and their social station. He recorded the name of each child and made a note of every sick person. Within his first three weeks, Newman recounted in a letter to his mother that he had visited the homes of one third of the parish. He was delighted with the warm reception he received. 'It will be a great thing done; I will be known by my parishioners and know them.' His mother replied in a letter the following week offering topics for future sermons. Newman responded, 'I take the hint.'

Newman organised Sunday school and large crowds listened to his sermons. Although he spoke in a quiet voice and without any theatrical flourishes, his style was a welcome contrast to that of the elderly Reverend Gutch. When people excused themselves to Newman for not attending church on Sundays, they blamed Reverend Gutch's weak voice or the lack of space in the overcrowded church. Newman set about making sure the new church would be built quickly. Land was given by Sir John Locke at Hacklingcroft Meadow and the architect, Daniel Robertson, built the church in Norman revival style. It was completed between 1827 and 1828, by which time Newman had left the parish.

Just two months after he began in the parish, Newman was summoned to London, where his father had taken ill. He spent several days at home, reading from the scriptures to his ailing parent. On 29 September 1824 John Newman died at the age of fifty-nine. The following week his eldest son presided at the funeral service. He recorded how much he admired his father and appreciated the sound advice he always gave him.

With the family in financial difficulties, Newman asked the father of his best friend, John W. Bowden, to help his brother Charles, who had not had the opportunity of a university education. Bowden senior found Charles a job as a clerk in the Bank of England, which provided him with an annual income of £80. His good fortune did not last and by 1832 Charles was dismissed from his post after several acrimonious letters to the directors of the bank. Thereafter he took to teaching, earning less money and growing increasingly eccentric.

On 27 March 1825 Newman was appointed by Whately as

Vice-Principal of St Alban's Hall, adjacent to Merton College. Here he oversaw the undergraduates and ensured that that they adhered to the college regulations. His mother shared his joy at the promotion. Writing to her daughter she told her the news. 'Were it anyone but John I should fear it would be too much for his heart or his head at so early an age, but in him I have the comforting anticipation that he will use his power for the benefit of those who entrust him with it; he will not be high-minded.' Several months later, Newman displayed his financial acumen as he wrote to his mother with evident pleasure that he had reconciled the annual accounts of £5,000 to the nearest few shillings.

In spring Newman presented himself to the Bishop of Oxford as a candidate and was accepted for Holy Orders. The ordination ceremony took place at Christchurch Cathedral on 29 May 1825. Almost immediately he had his first pastoral contretemps. The parish choir rebelled and resigned and by early June the congregation had to provide all the music, a situation that did not please the new minister. During the summer his mother and sisters stayed at the house of Dr Whately, who had departed for two months' vacation. Newman dedicated himself to entries for the *Encyclopaedia Metropolitana* and in September he spent a week with John Bowden on the Isle of Wight.

The death of John Newman had led to a sudden and dramatic change in the family fortunes. As the eldest, John Henry took responsibility, as was the custom of the time, for his mother and siblings. His earnings were meagre but he tried, as best he could, to support them with advice and any financial help he could. The first challenge was to find his mother and sisters a home, and he recommended that his mother take a house in Brighton. She still had money through her family and this relieved some pressure. Throughout his life, John Henry displayed deep affection for his mother, whose favourite son he was, and his sisters. However, when his mother expressed a wish to see her son married, John Henry replied that he believed he would die either 'within college walls or as a missionary'. He was less attached to his brothers, from whom he was separated by temperament and talents.

On his birthday, 21 February 1826, Newman was appointed college chaplain, a role that required both his regular attendance for worship and preaching. He was obliged to resign his positions at St Alban's Hall and St Clement's for this more prestigious position. Newman was assigned a room above the ante-chapel. The room, formerly used by Richard Whately as a larder, was adapted by Newman as a small oratory where he prayed, disturbed only by footsteps from the quad below. Whately entrusted Newman with the task of making a handwritten copy of his *Methods of Composition*, which he published in 1828.

Although he had enjoyed his experience at St Clement's, Newman was relieved that the appointment had come to an end as he needed all his time to care for the undergraduates for whom he was now responsible. In June 1826, Francis Newman graduated with a double first in Classics and, five months later, on 29 November, he was elected a fellow of Balliol College. It appeared that the two brothers were destined to pass their lives in academia.

Newman noted in his diary that people came to him for friendship and that he did not seek them out. He prized friendship and was upset when such relationships did not work out as he had wished, noting that 'they came to my great joy, they went to my great grief'. The academic circle of Oxford, which comprised some thirty colleges, could be claustrophobic. Newman forged a number of close friendships, often quite intense, with colleagues. He was careful not to commit his feelings to paper and the letters give a clear understanding of the relationship Newman had with each correspondent.

The young Newman was scarcely ten years older than his youngest student. He wrote to his mother that he 'had a great undertaking in the role of tutorship', adding that 'there was always danger of the love of literary pursuits assuming too prominent a place in the thought of a college tutor, or of his viewing his situation merely as a secular office'. His students generally found him both approachable and knowledgeable about current affairs, and many were in awe of his intellect. With his peers, most of whom were a few years older, he enjoyed mutual respect. A contemporary remarked that he was of a slight build and had a prominent nose. A close acquaintance, James Anthony Froude, stated that his face had an uncanny similarity to busts of Julius Caesar. Others noted simply that he was of average height and walked quickly.

The accumulation of writing contracts and educating a small number of students allowed Newman to live a more comfortable life. He was able to afford a servant, as was the habit in Oriel, and the luxury of buying his own books. Soon his savings in the bank began to grow. From these he put aside money to assist his mother, prepare dowries for his sisters and pay for his younger brother's education. He paid for the boarding house fees for his mother and sisters, who moved regularly between relatives and boarding houses. With an annual income of £600–700 per annum, he was able to augment his mother's income of £150, interest accrued from a sum his father left on his death.

From this time onwards, Newman often noted in his diary a need to avoid vanity in his intellectual abilities and to remain humble. Such diary entries continued into old age as he prays to God not to seek after 'a good name and reputation amongst men'.

In 1826 a new fellow was elected, one whose short life was to have a marked impact on Newman. Twenty-three-year-old Richard Hurrell Froude had graduated from Oriel with a double second in Classics and mathematics. The following year he was appointed a tutor, which brought him into closer contact with Newman. The two came to know each other well while writing articles for the *Encylopaedia Metropolitana*. There was a sense of pride and excitement in seeing their work published in a prestigious edition, and also delight in producing something novel. The pair struck up a close relationship as they were close in age and both interested in religion, while the other fellows were more interested in politics and philosophy. Speaking later about his relationship with Hurrell Froude, Newman remarked, in the manner that some Victorians adopted of speaking in the third person, that he 'felt more powerful than all others to which he had been subjected'.

On 1 May Newman decided that he would spend the next several months systematically reading the Fathers of the Church, a decision that had unexpected consequences. Study of patristics had not been highly regarded by academics in the Anglican tradition and there was little precedent to follow. A month later, he preached his first university sermon.

One of the subjects of conversation among the fellows at the dining table was the traditions of the Church. Dr Hawkins aired his belief that the Church developed the doctrine of the Bible in a gradual manner. This might have seemed obvious, but the Anglican Church had laid enormous emphasis on the Bible as the word of God, which needed no intermediary and no interpretation. The concept, enunciated by Martin Luther as *sola scriptura*, meant that the words of the Bible alone were understood as the word of God. Newman noted his reactions in his diary. If Hawkins was right, how did doctrine develop and, indeed, who was responsible for it?

Theological conversations formed only a small part of the dinner or post-dinner conversation. Whately had a peculiar habit of contorting his legs and placing his foot in his companion's lap while others soon succumbed to the effects of the excellent port. The prosecution of the Anglo-Ashanti war in West Africa, the appointment of the Duke of Wellington as commander-in-chief of the armed forces and later as prime minister, Sir Robert Peel's criminal law legislation, the establishment of St David's College at Lampeter in Wales and King's College London were all discussed. There was undoubtedly conversation about the Sacramental Test Act 1828, which removed the bar on non-Conformists and Catholics holding public office. Catholics were held in low regard by most Anglicans, who saw their 'popish ways' as remnants of medieval superstition shaken off by the majority of the English thanks to the sixteenth-century reformation of the Church. The old faith had been almost obliterated and Anglicans controlled nearly every level of society.

Newman gave an amusing account of one meal. A stranger had come into the dining hall. Following convention, Newman could not initiate the conversation as he had not been introduced by a third party. He records, 'We preserved an amicable silence, conversing with our teeth.'

Newman received an important nod of approval from Dr Howley, Bishop of London, who appointed him one of the preachers at Whitehall in 1827. In that same year, Newman was assigned the position of examiner in Classics for honours students. His career had taken off.

Personal tragedy struck the Newman family in January 1828. In the first days of the month Newman's sister Maria, then aged nineteen, began to feel unwell. Her situation deteriorated rapidly and, on 5 January, she died at home, of an unidentifed illness. The bereavement was devastating and Newman felt the loss deeply. Fifty years later, writing to his sister Jemima, he recalled how deeply he felt the loss of his cheerful and kind-hearted young sister, who had always been his favourite sibling. After the funeral he returned to Oxford to begin the new term with a heavy heart. Before he left London he paid for her tombstone. He commemorated her with a poem.

In February 1828 the post of provost at Oriel College fell vacant and Dr Edward Hawkins stood for election, narrowly beating Edward Pusey, the Regius Professor of Hebrew. Newman liked his colleague Pusey, commenting that if they wanted an angel as provost, Pusey would have had his vote. Later he defended his support for Hawkins, noting that Pusey played an important role in the future of the Church. 'If there had been no Pusey, there would have been no Movement, no Tracts, no Library of the Fathers.'

Newman admired Hawkins as an academic, although he soon disagreed with him on political and disciplinary issues. Newman and two other tutors argued that their role was not only to prepare undergraduates for their baccalaureate but also, as clergymen, to offer spiritual advice and guidance. Hawkins disagreed, indicating that this approach would allow personal preference and favouritism to enter the relationship. The issue was not so severe that Hawkins could justify removing Newman as one of the four college tutors. Instead, as each student graduated he was not replaced, eventually leaving Newman with no pupils. It was a genteel way of ousting Newman and it also reduced his income.

Hawkins had been vicar of the University Church of St Mary the Virgin on Oxford High Street and when he was elected provost, the appointment fell to Newman. St Mary's was a stone's throw from Oriel College and had had links with Oriel since the fourteenth century. It had housed the university's first library. In 1555 it had been the site of the trial of the Oxford martyrs. Archbishop Thomas Cranmer was tried for heresy and burned to death nearby. Wesley had preached a memorable sermon there condemning the laxity of the university staff and students. Unsurprisingly, he was not asked back.

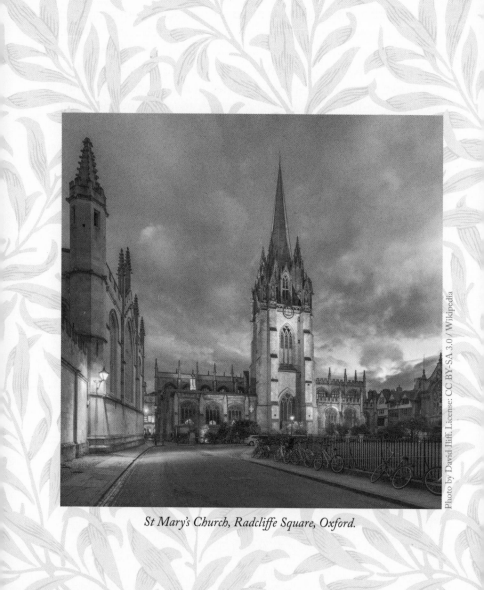

St Mary's Church, Radcliffe Square, Oxford.

CHAPTER 3:
VICAR AT ST MARY'S

The position at St Mary's was Newman's most prestigious to date. He resigned his chaplaincy at Oriel in order to concentrate on preparing his sermons. The church had been refurbished the previous year with the addition of extra seating galleries, an organ screen and a newly carved pulpit. Within a few months the new vicar's sermons became popular among the students of the university. One student, William Lockhart, later recalled, 'It was as if we heard the voice of God speaking for the first time.' The position of vicar was usually held for several years; Newman remained at St Mary's until 1843. It provided him with financial security and a vicarage in which to reside. However, while some appreciated his sermons, others were appalled by his gradual leaning towards 'superstition' and 'popish idolatry'.

The position raised Newman's profile in the colleges but, more importantly, it prompted him to revise his preaching method and to include quotations of the early Fathers to whose writings he was now paying particular attention. Newman's sermons were popular and upwards of 500 undergraduates attended Sunday services to hear him preach. For several years there had been a movement to repeal anti-Catholic legislation, particularly the prohibition on the election of Catholics to parliament. In 1829 the Roman Catholic Relief Act was passed, allowing Catholics to sit in parliament. Newman showed little interest in the role of Catholics at the time, although his theological leanings were bringing him imperceptibly closer to Catholicism.

University in the early nineteenth century was largely for the elite. British society was organised on class lines and there was little movement between the strata. Usually friends made at university became colleagues in any future career. In 1829 the Mozley family visited members who had enrolled to study at Oxford. They recalled meeting Newman, then young Thomas Mozley's tutor. Newman struck up a friendship with Thomas's sister Anne, a relationship that would endure for the rest of their lives, Newman eventually entrusting her with the preparation of his letters for publication.

In early 1830, Newman received a letter from Hugh Rose, a Cambridge-educated academic, with a request to provide a volume for the Bishop of London's *Theological Library* on the Arian controversy of the fourth century, an event to which Reformation theology had paid scant attention. It was an area in which Newman had already acquired a certain expertise.

The controversy between two ancient presbyters hardly offered an exciting investigation. However, Arius and Athanasius, both clerics in Alexandria in Egypt, caused the first great split in the Christian Church and threatened to destroy the entire Christian community. In 319, Arius (253–336), a native of Libya and a presbyter of Alexandria, addressed a letter to the Patriarch Alexander in which he argued that Jesus was created by God and therefore had not existed for eternity. He was a human infused with the divine presence in a unique way, but he was not God. For Arius, it was heresy to compare Jesus to God and any attempt to do so was to strip God of his unique status.

Athanasius (296/8–373), a native of Egypt, was in his early twenties when the controversy broke out and was some forty years younger than Arius. He countered Arius's claim and argued that Jesus had two natures, human and divine. Thus Jesus was neither simply God wearing a human mask nor a human clothed with divinity, but fully God and man. The patriarch convened a synod at Alexandria in 321 which condemned Arius's teaching and deposed him from office.

The depth of feeling stirred up among ordinary people is captured in the writings of a contemporary: 'Ask a baker for a loaf of bread and he will tell you how the Father is greater than the Son. Try to buy some fish and the fisherwoman will tell you that the Son is obedient to the Father. There is nothing but madness in the city.' Sailors in the Egyptian port sang sea shanties that Arius had composed for them.

Such was the consternation spreading across the north of Africa and into Palestine that Emperor Constantine summoned the bishops of the Church to meet in Nicaea, a seaside town in modern-day Turkey. Constantine had embraced Christianity in 313, when he attributed his success against Maxentius at the Battle of the Milvian Bridge to Christ. Constantine had no desire to see his new religion rent asunder by faction fighting.

Over 200 bishops assembled in early June, the first time such a large gathering had been convened. Taking his place on the imperial dais, the purple-clad emperor addressed the bishops: 'Dissent within the church is worse than war.' The emperor demanded that the bishops immediately resolve the issue and restore unity. The bishops formulated the Nicene Creed but, while all signed the document, not all were happy with the manner in which the issue had been concluded. When Patriarch Alexander died in 327, Athanasius was elected by the clergy and people to succeed him. However, controversy continued to plague him and he was denounced to the emperor, who sent him into exile.

Newman read with interest of the vicissitudes of the orthodox Athanasius and his fight, as it seemed, against the whole world. He faced five violent exiles before his death in his mid-seventies. St Jerome praised his courage in the face of imperial persecution and fraternal betrayal, claiming that 'he snatched the whole world from the jaws of Satan'.

The controversy left a deep impression on Newman. Writing some years later in his *Apologia Pro Vita Sua* he observed, 'I saw clearly that in the history of Arianism, the pure Arians were the Protestants, the semi-Arians were the Anglicans and Rome now was what it was then.'

Newman exchanged his views with other fellows at Oriel and in broader Church circles. Edward Pusey, who increasingly exerted influence on his fellow Anglican divines who sought change within the Church, was in agreement with Newman. Although Semitic languages were Pusey's first interest, the scholar began to take a more active interest in the thought of the early theologians of the Church. It was through Pusey that Newman became acquainted with contemporary German theologians.

Newman was so fascinated by the Arian controversy that he decided to write a book on the subject. He wanted to contribute to an area he believed was little understood within the Church of England. Far from being a dusty subject for academics, he believed that study would help people deepen their understanding of the true nature of Jesus.

As Newman had no students he had ample time to devote to his parochial duties and his writing, and in 1832 he published *The Arians of the Fourth Century*. At the end of that year he joined Richard Hurrell Froude and his father, the archdeacon, on a trip to the Mediterranean. The young man had been ill with tuberculosis for some months and a holiday in a warmer climate was regarded as preferable to the cold winter in England. The journey provided Newman with a welcome break from the stressful preceding years and it also gave him an excuse to be absent from Oxford. By now it was clear to Newman's colleagues that Hawkins had no intention of assigning students to Newman's care and this may have persuaded Newman to accept the invitation to escape to the continent.

The trio sailed on the *Hermès* across the Bay of Biscay, down through the Straits of Gibraltar, to Malta, the Ionian islands, Sicily, Naples and Rome. Richard cheerfully noted in his diary that Newman was regularly seasick and continued writing letters, sometimes several in a day, to his mother and sisters. In his diary Newman noted with distaste the Mediterranean forms of Catholicism. It was his first exposure to a culture outside

England and in his letters home he indicated how overwhelmed he felt by the change of food and circumstances. While he rarely entered a church, he was appalled by the religious processions and statues that abounded and the unattractive music. Hurrell Froude was less offended by the places they visited, but in his diary observed that Catholics were 'queer folk'.

After four months, Richard and his father went back to England while Newman decided to return to Sicily. Shortly after arriving on the island at Leonforte in mid-April, he contracted typhoid fever. When the doctor was summoned, he could communicate only in Latin. He became so weak that he thought he would die and gave instructions to his servant Gennaro about how to contact his family and friends to inform them of his demise. Gennaro successfully nursed Newman through his illness and he gradually recovered. He later stated that he felt God had some work for him in England, although he did not know what it might be. On 13 June, while still recuperating, he sailed from Palermo on a cargo ship loaded with oranges, bound for Marseilles. Delayed by rough seas, the ship was becalmed off the French coast. While waiting for the weather to change, Newman penned the poem 'Lead, Kindly Light'.

His brush with death, as he believed, made a deep impression on Newman, and he later reflected on it in a short pamphlet published as *Illness in Sicily*. Here he explained how he felt God was fighting against him for his self-will and clearly reproached himself for abandoning his friend and his father on their return to England.

There is a noticeable change in the tone of Newman's writing after he arrived home on 9 July; he repeatedly expressed a new confidence in God's providence. Having visited his mother and sisters, he returned to Oxford. On 14 July, Reverend John Keble preached a forceful sermon entitled *National Apostasy*. There was immediate reaction to the provocative words and it ultimately led to the formation of the Tractarian movement, aimed at a fresh look at the tradition of the apostles.

The Catholic Emancipation Act was passed in 1829 and the following year the Whigs won the election and formed a government under Prime Minister Robert Peel. The Catholic Emancipation Act was passed less to help Catholics than to win their hitherto untapped and substantial votes. The Whigs presented themselves as a party of reform and immediately tackled a number of administrative issues. Peel skilfully engaged the support of the bishops. He gathered together five bishops and seven senior politicians, inviting them to dinner in his house. One of problems discussed was the increasing number of non-Conformists, Christians who were not Anglicans. These included Methodists and Presbyterians. Despite the passing of the Catholic Emancipation Act, there was still significant opposition to Catholics playing any political role. The bishops were scarcely aware of the changes in opinion that were about to take place in the Anglican Church thanks to the work of a number of Oxford academics.

Following the provocative sermon on national apostasy, John Keble soon gathered around him other academics and clergymen who agreed with his fundamental thesis that the way out of the difficulties for the Anglican Church was to return to the doctrines of the pre-Reformation. The Church of England had preserved the orders of bishop, priest and deacon. Public worship had been maintained in the cathedrals and churches, where matins and evensong, remnants of the old monastic tradition, were regularly prayed. Newman was particularly disturbed when, in August 1833, the government passed the Church Temporalities (Ireland) Act, which reduced the number of Irish dioceses from twenty-two to twelve. This he perceived as the unacceptable interference of politicians in ecclesiastical affairs. He believed that no diocese, once founded, should cease to exist. In Oxford, the new power in Westminster forced several clergymen to re-examine the basis for the Anglican Church's authority. Did it rely on Christ, or on the government acting on behalf of the king?

Newman encouraged study of the early Church Fathers among his colleagues. The new-found interest found its way into the preaching of several clergymen. The sermons were published in pamphlets, or 'tracts', and were eagerly read. Newman himself travelled around Oxfordshire on horseback delivering packages of the tracts to enthusiastic readers, which led to the formation of the so-called 'Tractarian movement'.

Newman's first sermon addressed the issue of priesthood in the Anglican Church. He reminded the clergy that theirs was a vocation of prayer and service. Over the years since the Reformation, many of the clergy entered the Church simply because they were academic, or because they were younger sons who would not inherit the family estate. The first tract was short, just four pages, but it caught public attention. Over the next eight years Keble, Newman, Froude, Pusey and a Worcester don, William Palmer, were to compose ninety 'tracts', in which they examined various themes. What were the effects of baptism? What happened to the consecrated elements of bread and wine at the Eucharist? Were the reforms of Henry VIII and Elizabeth I valid? Could the Church of England embrace the teachings of the Early Fathers? Did sacramental confession exist in the Church? All these questions marked changes from Anglican practice at the time. In the twenty-nine tracts Newman wrote between 1833 and February 1841, he tried to bring the Anglican Church back, as he saw it, to its Catholic roots.

There were also college politics to consider. Keble had retired some years earlier and Newman had recently resigned his position as tutor at Oriel. But the others risked their livelihoods if they continued to challenge the academic status quo. An example of such a challenge was the Tractarians' unsuccessful opposition to the appointment of Renn Dickson Hampden as Regius Professor of Divinity. Newman was too fully engaged in his parochial duties to worry unduly over academic jealousies and squabbles. Encouraged by university students and friends, he began to publish his sermons annually, developing his views.

As Oxford continued to expand, Newman was faced with his second church-building enterprise. The parish of St Mary's was growing and a chapel of ease was required in the area of Littlewood, less than three miles from Oxford. Newman approached the authorities at Oriel for permission to build a church but was refused as funds were lacking and the area was too poor to resource a new building. Newman was irritated by the lack of support and rented a room in the district where he could teach religion to children. He continued to agitate for a church and organised a petition among the landowners and local inhabitants. In April 1835 his sisters Jemima and Harriet collected signatures in the parish for a petition to erect a chapel of ease, which Newman presented to the university authorities. Oriel College agreed to the new building but made a proviso that Newman had to raise the bulk of the money himself.

Newman had connections to a few wealthy individuals, and his mother and family, despite their limited resources, supported the effort financially. Bristol-born architect H. J. Underwood was engaged to design a church in the Early English style. Newman invited his mother to lay the foundation stone on 21 July 1835, and the church was consecrated on 22 September 1836, by Richard Bagot, Bishop of Oxford. Close to the west door, Newman placed three plaques commemorating the generosity of the benefactors, who included, among others, Edward Hawkins, John and Thomas Keble, the friends and family of John Bowden, Thomas Mozley, Matthew Bloxam and his sisters. The total cost was about £700.

As vicar of St Mary's, Newman could not look after the church, so he arranged for the appointment of John Rouse Bloxam, a fellow of Magdalen College, as curate. It was an inspired choice as Bloxam was sympathetic to the aims of the Tractarians and delighted in the rituals of the emerging Anglo-Catholic tradition. He had been instrumental in restoring a four-hundred-year-old tradition of welcoming in the month of May from the college tower. The choir of boys and undergraduates, dressed in red cassocks and white surplices, sang the *Hymnus Eucharisticus* from the roof of the tower at six in the morning. At the end they threw roses and lilies to the crowd gathered below. During his time as curate Bloxam corresponded with the influential convert Ambrose Lisle March Phillips de Lisle on the unification of the Anglican and Catholic Churches.

While building Littlewood church and administering the parish of St Mary, Newman continued his study of the early Church Fathers. In the summer of 1836, Pusey announced his intention of compiling 'An Oxford Library of the Fathers of the Holy Catholic Church, Anterior to the Division of the East and West'. The work, to be published in instalments, would enlist the talents of his fellow academics. Newman signed up enthusiastically. The Archbishop of Canterbury, William Howley, lent his support. The subscription, which grew to 3,700 supporters, ensured its success.

That same year Pusey published an *Ernest Remonstrance*, a riposte to the anonymous *The Pope's Pastoral Letter*, which purported to be from the pope. It was the first time Pusey combatted anti-Catholic feeling. Newman was grateful for his influence among the Tractarians, observing 'that without him we would have been a mob'. As time went by, Newman and several academics became increasingly convinced that the Anglican Church would have to return to its Catholic basics. The question was simply how to achieve the aim. While Pusey believed the earlier, authentic traditions within the Anglican Communion could be restored, others contemplated converting to the Church of Rome.

The year 1836 was an emotional one for Newman. On 28 February his dear friend, Richard Hurrell Froude, succumbed to tuberculosis and, three months later, on 17 May, Newman's mother died in her home at Littlemore near Oxford. She and her daughters had become volunteers in John Henry's parish, although Mrs Newman remarked that she 'found the parish very High Church'. Newman had lost his most treasured confidante.

The Newman sisters married two brothers in 1836. On 27 April Jemima married James Mozley and on 27 September Harriet married Thomas Mozley. That same year Charles had confided in John Henry that he was ready to be reconciled with his brother. He had wandered from one job to another and failed to keep any for long. Neither brother had spoken to the other for several years. The reconciliation did not last long, and in 1837, Newman saw his brother for the last time. Charles went to live in France where he found a job as an usher, or teaching assistant, but was dismissed when he attacked a pupil and bit his ear. He then flitted from job to job, always short of money, and Newman and Francis supported him financially for many years. The rift was a cause of anguish to Newman. There was only a year's age difference. Many years later, he described his brother's life as 'aimless, profitless and forlorn'.

John Henry Newman & Ambrose St John, no later than 1875.

CHAPTER 4:
CONVERSION TO CATHOLICISM

In his autobiography, Newman identified 1839 as the pivotal year in which he turned away from the Anglican Church towards Rome. He recalled during the long vacation reading about the Monophysites in Coptic Egypt, who believed that Jesus had one single nature, in contrast with the definition of the Council of Nicaea, which declared that Jesus had two natures, human and divine. On 30 July he recounted to a friend his 'doubts about the tenableness of Anglican tenets'. He came to believe that the Anglican Church was heretical. Rome, on the other hand, had never changed.

In 1838, an Oxford scholar, William Palmer of Worcester College, published a seminal book, *The Origins of the Church of Christ*, in which he proposed a branch theory of Church. The two Newman brothers were friendly with Palmer and had briefly shared lodgings with him. According to Palmer, each Church, Catholic, Orthodox and Anglican, possessed the essential truths of the Christian faith. These branches are called to grow and come together to form the Church willed by Christ. Newman liked Palmer's thought and was attracted by the idea of growth towards eventual union of the three Churches.

Tract 90 sealed the fate of John Henry Newman as a member of the Established Church in England. In the sermon he tried to argue that the Anglican Church, faithful to the Thirty-Nine Articles, was essentially in accord with the decrees of the Council of Trent. It was, in other words, fundamentally Catholic.

This was a step too far for the Anglican bishops, who were infuriated by the preaching of what they saw as a pretentious cleric. The Council of Trent, held in three sessions between

1545 and 1563, was an attempt to reform the Catholic Church in the light of the criticism of Protestant theologians such as Luther, Calvin and Zwingli. The Thirty-Nine Articles had been formulated at the same time that the Council was taking place and contained the essential doctrines of the Church of England. It was a stretch of the imagination to claim that the decrees of the Council of Trent could harmonise with the Thirty-Nine Articles. The reaction to Tract 90 was severely hostile. The four tutors of Balliol wrote a scathing response to the tracts in general, accusing the members of the movement of being Catholics in disguise. In the spring of 1841 Newman was ordered by the Bishop of Oxford to desist from spreading his views and cease as a member of the Oxford Movement.

Newman increasingly found himself at variance with his Anglican colleagues. He could be acidic and several clergymen now avoided him. In his autobiographical *Apologia* he wrote, 'I dare say I gave offence to both and I am not here defending it.'

During the festivities to mark the dedication of John Keble's new parish church at Amfield in Hursley on 21 April 1841, Newman met a recently ordained Anglican cleric, Ambrose St John, a graduate of Christchurch, Oxford, who had studied Syriac and Hebrew under Pusey. He had been a student of Samuel Wilberforce, a fellow at Oriel with Newman some years earlier. The twenty-five-year-old was curate with Wilberforce at Bransgore in Hampshire. Although St John was fourteen years younger than him, Newman was drawn to his extrovert personality and the two men immediately struck up a friendship. They corresponded for a period of months, discussing semantics and the state of the Anglican Church. The younger man was clearly impressed by the senior cleric, who had earned a high reputation in the academic and pastoral fields.

The changes in the Anglican Church were becoming intolerable to Newman. On 11 November 1841 he wrote a long letter to the Archbishop of Canterbury enumerating the errors and mistakes of the Anglican Communion and its dangerous alliance with the teachings of Luther and Calvin. He realised the gravity of what his offensive letter had done and described himself as on his 'deathbed'. There were sure to be repercussions, and he awaited them with a certain amount of trepidation. None came.

In April 1842, Newman moved to an old coach house in Littlemore that belonged to the Oxford and Cambridge Coach company. The stables and grain store were converted into small rooms, each with a bed, desk, chair and chest of drawers. The vicar installed his library in the barn and was soon joined by several friends who were drawn to share a semi-monastic life of prayer and study. The young men transformed the buildings by joining them together with a veranda. A curate had been appointed to St Mary's two years previously and this had given Newman increased time for study and the contemplative prayer to which he felt increasingly drawn.

Newman was very happy in this new setting. The company of enthusiastic young academics and clerics was congenial. A cook and maid looked after lodgings while the young guests did some building work and converted the courtyard into a garden. Newman acquired thirteen Latin breviaries and the little community began to recite the Divine Office. He had commenced praying the Catholic Divine Office in Latin in 1836. Throughout the week the group met with Newman for 'conferences' in which they discussed issues in theology. He also offered individual spiritual direction. He wanted to establish the way of life he had wanted for his Oriel students. There was ample time to study and write and think out his developing views. In his correspondence Newman indicated how helpful he found these 'colloquia'. Increasingly discussion turned towards restoring the Catholicity of the ancient faith within Anglicanism.

On Sunday, 7 August 1843, Ambrose St John arrived at Littlemore, with the intention of staying three months. Newman delightedly welcomed the young man and assigned him a room and daily duties. By now Newman was convinced that he could no longer remain as a minister of the Church of England and, on 18 September, he formally resigned as vicar of St Mary's. He had preached some 600 sermons at the church, and over almost two decades had established himself among the foremost theological experts at Oxford.

Writing some years later, Newman marvelled that he had not converted from the Anglican Church many years earlier. He reproached himself for using the parish for his own ends. The church was the university chapel but the people had a right to a good vicar who would care for their needs. As early as 1839 Newman had written to a friend asking for advice as to how to proceed. He admitted that while he did carry out his duties as best he could, he also felt that he was turning the church into a 'university office'.

In September 1841 Newman embarked on a series of short biographies of the saints of England, to be published in eight small volumes. He simultaneously wrote *The Development of Christian Doctrine*, one of his most influential works, exploring the way in which theologians contributed to the development of the Church. As he developed his thought he became increasingly uncomfortable in the Anglican communion.

On Sunday, 25 September 1843, the church at Littlemore was packed for the anniversary service of thanksgiving for the dedication of the church. As was his custom, Newman gave the annual sermon. This, however, was to be his last as an Anglican clergyman. The sermon was later published as *The Parting of Friends*. As he descended from the pulpit, he removed his preaching stole from his shoulders and laid it on the altar rails. It was the last time he participated in a service in the Anglican Church. Many wept openly as they realised that this silent gesture signalled the vicar's imminent departure.

Newman continued to live at Littlemore. While he no longer had a direct role in the parish, he continued to be respected by the families that had come to know him well and understood the strange path upon which he had embarked.

As late as 23 February 1841 Newman had written to his good friend John Keble, 'No one could have a more unfavourable view of the present state of Roman Catholics.' Yet within the space of four and a half years he had completely changed his mind.

On 24 September 1843, the Feast of St John the Baptist, a visitor arrived to see one of the Littlemore residents, John Dalgairns. Fr Dominic Barbieri, a member of the Passionist Congregation, was a highly regarded preacher and had a reputation for making converts. The pair visited Newman in his room and spoke for a while. In his diary entry that evening Newman wrote, 'Father Dominic called.' He was already familiar with the Italian priest, who had received many Anglicans into the Catholic Church. Within days, Newman made the same decision, almost certainly impelled by the conversion of several friends, most notably Ambrose St John, who had been received into the Church on 3 October at Priory Park in Bath.

There was pressure from the authorities at Oriel College and Newman clearly could not expect to hold on to his fellowship. On 5 October 1845, he wrote to the college, resigning as a fellow.

Three nights later, Fr Barbieri came to Littlemore. Newman indicated that it was a chance visit but it is possible that he had asked Barbieri for the very purpose of being received into the Catholic Church. The priest arrived shortly before midnight. Despite the late hour, the pair talked into the night and Newman made what he called a Confession of the sins of his life. He wrote a short letter to his sister Jemima, informing her of his intention to be received into the Catholic Church by Fr Barbieri the following day. He said he knew the news would not please her.

On the evening of 9 October 1845, in the company of two other residents of Littlemore, he made his profession of faith before Fr Barbieri and was received, with conditional baptism, into the Church. For Newman this was a homecoming, 'for I was a ship that finally came to port', and he always referred to it as 'my day'.

News of Newman's conversion to Catholicism spread rapidly throughout the British Isles. On 13 October 1845 *The Tablet*, Great Britain's premier Catholic paper, published the news. Although the writer professed to have little knowledge of Mr Newman's conversion, he wrote at length of the move's importance to both the Anglican and Catholic Churches. Some sensed that the conversion of Newman and his companions was the beginning of a veritable tidal wave that would restore England as 'Our Lady's Bower'.

Among the first Catholic bishops to recognise the importance of Newman's conversion was Nicholas Wiseman. Born in the Spanish town of Seville to Irish parents, Wiseman had studied for the priesthood and at the age of twenty-seven had been appointed rector of the Venerable English College in Rome. He had been ordained by Pope Gregory XIV in 1840 as coadjutor bishop to Thomas Walsh of the Central District of the English Midlands and rector of Oscott College, the regional seminary. Wiseman, who had confirmed Newman three weeks after his baptism, understood the new convert well. On 24 November he invited Newman and his Catholic companions to move to Oscott. Writing to his friend James Hope, Newman explained, 'He thinks such a community, cultivating Sacred Scripture, and acting in missions and the like through England, according to the calling for each, is the best chance for the conversion of our country'.

Newman spent his forty-fifth birthday at Littlemore. He had reluctantly decided to take up Wiseman's offer and leave the little community. He left the next day, Sunday, 22 February. The parting was painful. Although he maintained a correspondence with several parishioners he did not visit the place where he had lived so happily for another thirty-two years.

The personal sacrifice in terms of friendship and family relations was something that he had underestimated. Many fellow colleagues cut him off completely. When Newman wrote to his sister Jemima on the eve of his conversion, she replied that 'it was if a friend might die'. His sister Harriet did not reply to his letters and mutual friends told him of her disgust. Francis, by now Professor of Classics at Manchester New College and a prolific author, wrote disapprovingly of his brother's defection.

The adjustment was difficult for everybody, especially students and parishioners, and Newman was grateful to those who supported him. By August his family had still not forgiven the abrupt separation. Writing to his sister Jemima, he vented his hurt. 'When my great trial came, my own relations, and they only, were those who could find the heart, or lack of reverence, to write censoriously to me.'

Newman was under no illusions about the enormity of his decision. 'I am going to those whom I do not know and of whom I expect very little. I am making myself an outcast, and that at my age.' But the conversion was dictated by his conscience. He later observed, 'But here below, to grow is to change and to be perfect means to have changed often.'

CHAPTER 5:
BECOMING A CATHOLIC PRIEST

John Henry Newman

Newman discussed his future and the possibility of becoming a priest with Wiseman, who suggested that he, and some others, spend a year studying at the Pontifical Gregorian College, founded by St Ignatius Loyola. It would have the added advantage of exposing him to current theological developments on the Continent. The new converts agreed and Newman made preparations to travel to Rome with St John in October, a year after his conversion.

This second journey through Europe was far more enjoyable than the visit he had made with the Froudes more than a decade earlier. Wiseman had provided letters to various prelates en route through France, Switzerland and Italy, recommending the pair to their hospitality. In the north of France Newman and St John visited the Archbishop of Paris, the papal nuncio and the Bishop of Langres. Newman was appalled at the ghastly tea and coffee served in tiny cups. The meal times bewildered him and more than once the irregular timetable caused him an upset stomach. He noted wryly that the hosts are 'in utter astonishment that the fare disagrees with us'. A feather bed at Langres caused him sleepless nights and he longed for the straw mattress of Littlemore. Clearly Newman appreciated the fuss, even though he feigned to be aghast at the food. 'The clergy are a merry, simple, affectionate set – some of them quite touchingly kind and warm-hearted towards me.' He was amused at the number of times they bowed. 'They have never done bowing in the most formal manner. St John has asked in vain how often we ought to bow when taking leave – as for me, who hardly ever made a formal bow in my life, I can hardly keep my countenance as I put my elbows to my hips and make a segment of a circle, the lower vertebra being the circle and my head the circumference.'

The party stayed with the Archbishop of Besançon. Newman was impressed with his fluency in Latin and the fact that he offered afternoon tea as soon as they arrived. Mentioning his fondness for the Dominicans, the archbishop immediately dissuaded Newman from any thoughts of joining the order. 'It is the business of you all to put yourselves under your Bishop and be regulated by him in all that you do.'

In Italy, Wiseman's introductions continued to work their magic. Milan was Newman's favourite city to date. Writing to William Wilberforce, he spoke glowingly about the beauty of the city's architecture and, in a letter to William Goodenough, an Oxford convert, he referred to St Charles Borromeo who, 'in his day had saved his country from Protestantism and its collateral evils ... as we are now attempting to do something to resist the same foes of the Church in England'. From there they set off for Rome, arriving in the last week of October 1846, and moved into the College of Propaganda Fidei, close to the Piazza di Spagna, on 9 November. Wiseman again used his network of acquaintances and furnished the students with letters of introduction to his old Roman friends.

The months spent in Rome were far more pleasant than Newman's earlier sojourn in 1834. Although at forty-five he was twice the age of most of the other seminarians at the Gregorian College, he enjoyed the relative anonymity of the Eternal City. He observed the city's rhythms, from the calling of the Angelus bell to the raucous devotional hymns that accompanied processions and fiestas. The embroidered silks and sumptuous vestments of the clergy glinting in churches illuminated by candlelight caught his eye. A competent musician who played both the viola and organ, he listened to the cadences of Gregorian Chant and Renaissance polyphony.

The new pope had been elected some months earlier, on 16 June 1846. There was enormous interest in the election of the moderate Archbishop Giovanni Maria Mastai Ferretti, who had taken the name Pius IX. There were hopes in all quarters that he would be a unifying force across the Italian peninsula. Newman witnessed the *possessio,* the traditional ceremony during which the pope takes possession of his cathedral at the Lateran. He wrote approvingly of the colourful procession of the papal court as it made its way through the city, the pope sitting on his throne carried by attendants while the silk canopy swayed above his head and white ostrich-feather fans moved from side to side.

News of Newman's presence in Rome soon spread. The Jesuit theologian Giacomo Mazio, who had extensive contacts in the city, presented the celebrated convert to several important ecclesiastics. Five weeks after his conversion, Newman had published *An Essay On The Development Of Christian Doctrine,* arguing, as he had in some of his *Tracts for the Times,* that doctrine developed organically from the Bible. It was, for Newman, one of the principal reasons for becoming a Catholic. He believed that the Catholic Church had been the steward of the seed of the Gospel and had nurtured and fostered it, often at the expense of defending it from heresy.

To Newman's surprise, quite a few theologians in Rome were familiar with his work and thought. Several influential Catholic theologians, including the Jesuit Giovanni Perrone, supported the manner in which Newman had expounded his beliefs. Wiseman had advised Newman that the Jesuits were the principal academics in Rome, a view with which Newman concurred. Writing to his friend Richard Stanton, a priest of the London Oratory, he observed, 'There is no doubt the Jesuits are the real men in Rome ... they are the prominent men.'

The Roman School, in the ascendancy in the mid-nineteenth century, laid new emphasis on patristics and tradition, and this fitted well with Newman's thought. Some academics believed that the providential conversion of Newman would lead to a new spring of the Catholic Church in Britain and encouraged his endeavours. Several Dominicans, Franciscans and Jesuits were engaged in theological arguments about the proposition of Mary, the mother of Jesus. The debate centred around the question whether Mary was conceived with or without the stain of original sin. The theme had been debated since at least the early Middle Ages and rumour had it that Pope Pius wished to proclaim it as a dogma of the Church. Newman offered his views, but his area of study was not Marian and he was frustrated by the time that the Roman theologians were devoting to the question. His time in Rome was limited and he was anxious to make the most of whatever Catholic theology he could imbibe. He read a large number of Catholic theologians proposed by Perrone and composed a short unpublished work, *De Fide*, in which he examined the contribution of the scholastics to faith. As a mark of favour and in recognition of his conversion, Pope Pius conferred on Newman an honorary doctorate of divinity. There was no question about Newman's sincerity as a Catholic nor about his orthodoxy, and the papal honour was his vindication. During his time in Rome, a group of scholars suggested that Newman join in their plan to translate the Bible into contemporary English. Newman agreed but the project never got off the ground.

With ordination looming Wiseman and Newman discussed his immediate future. He was initially drawn to the Jesuits and Dominicans, while he also explored the Benedictine tradition. In Rome, he had become more familiar with the figure of the great sixteenth-century saint, Philip Neri (+1594), a Florentine who lived for many years in Rome and was referred to as the city's 'third Apostle', after St Peter and St Paul. The cheerful and generous Neri was remembered by Romans for his charitable acts and the education of children. Many priests associated themselves with Neri, who founded the Congregation of the Oratory.

In January 1847 Newman decided, along with his bosom friends, Ambrose St John and John Dalgairns, to become members of an Oratory, preferably one that they would set up in England.

It would allow them to live together in a small community of clerics and engage in study, teaching and parochial work. The structure would be somewhat reminiscent of Oxford days, in Oriel and later at Littlemore. 'The nearest approximation to an Oratorian Congregation that I know,' he said at the first chapter meeting of the priests, 'is one of the Colleges in the Anglican universities. Take such a College, destroy the Head's house, annihilate wife and children, restore him to his body of fellows, give the Head and fellows missionary work and you have a Congregation of St Philip before your eyes.'

Early on the morning of Sunday 30 May 1847 Newman and St John were ordained to the priesthood in the Chapel of the Three Kings at the Congregation of Propaganda Fidei by the Prefect, Cardinal Giacomo Filippo Fransoni. There was no family member present. Four days later Father Newman celebrated his first Mass in a Jesuit chapel. By autumn, he intended to return to England and begin a new chapter of his life.

Pope Pius IX.

CHAPTER 6:
THE ORATORY

In a private audience with Pope Pius shortly after his ordination, Newman discussed the idea of setting up an Oratory in England, with a view to forming the next generation of converts and to assist in the education of young Catholics.

In preparation for the establishment of the Oratory, Newman and six prospective candidates who had recently converted from Anglicanism gathered in the church of Santa Croce in Gerusalemme where they began a novitiate. The following month, Pope Pius called to visit the novices at Santa Croce and formally established the Oratory. In September, Newman wrote to Elizabeth Bowden, his friend John's widow, telling her that some of his university sermons were being translated into French and that he had been asked to write the preface.

Newman was appointed superior of the small community of the Oratory to be established in England. Pius prepared the bull of authorisation to re-establish the Catholic hierarchy in Great Britain, intending that Newman would carry it back to England. This would be a theatrical *coup de grâce*, the vision of an eminent Anglican convert bearing the pope's letter to restore the dioceses suppressed during the English Reformation. In the event the letter was not ready and the decision was deferred for several months. Before he left Rome, Newman received visits from Cardinal Fransoni and Cardinal Ostini of the Congregation for the Council. The Archbishop of Milan also called on Newman when he came to Rome to see the pope.

The group remained in Rome until December, when they returned to England to celebrate Christmas with their families before beginning the new way of life. Newman and St John travelled along the eastern coast of Italy and across the Alps into Bavaria, where they called on the celebrated Dr Johann Josef von Döllinger, a professor at Munich University. Newman had met Döllinger in 1836 when the Bavarian cleric had visited Oxford. The pair had kept up a correspondence, exchanging views in particular on the limits of papal authority. During this period, Newman composed his novel, *Loss and Gain,* which followed the life of a young Oxford undergraduate's conversion to Catholicism. The novel was, in part, a reflection of Newman's own experiences in Oxford some years earlier.

By early 1848 everything was in place for the new Oratory, which opened on 1 February at Old Oscott. The previous year Newman and converts in the Midlands had lost the important support of Nicholas Wiseman, who had been transferred to London to accompany Bishop Thomas Walsh. Wiseman's last act was to arrange for the transfer of Old Oscott to the new community, which Newman renamed Maryvale. Wiseman's future was uncertain and rumours circulated that he was to be made a cardinal and brought to Rome to replace Cardinal Acton. Newman publicly offered his congratulations to Wiseman but privately worried about the future and if the next bishop would prove as supportive.

Any concern that the new Oratory would not be successful soon evaporated. Newman wrote enthusiastically to William Wilberforce, now a convert, that the retreats were a huge success. Twenty-two people had been received into the Church and up to 600 people packed into the little chapel at Maryvale. With more priests joining the Oratory, Newman realised that he would soon be able, or forced, to open a second Oratory.

The opportunity came soon. A former Anglican clergyman, Frederick Faber, had converted and established a community at Cotton Hall in Staffordshire. He and his community applied to join the Oratory. By now Newman, despite his shy nature, had become a respected leader of his community. Although hesitant at first, Newman accepted the community but recommended that Faber and the new Oratorians settle in London. He may not have wished to accept an entire community that already had been led by Faber and he could count on Wiseman's support in finding a location for a London Oratory.

The changing political and religious situation in the British Isles was followed closely by the Roman Curia. The pope had fled to Gaeta two years earlier in 1848, the so-called Year of the Revolutions, when political unrest had swept across Europe.

The improving relations between the papacy and the British crown was underscored when Queen Victoria offered Pope Pius refuge in England or Malta, although the act of hospitality was because the pope was a monarch, not because he was the sovereign pontiff. Encouraged by the royal gesture, Pius decided that the time was right to restore the British hierarchy.

Rumours of Wiseman's promotion continued, and when he was summoned to Rome in mid-1850 to meet Pope Pius, he fully expected to receive an appointment within the Curia. To his surprise, the pope had decided to place Wiseman in London at the head of the new Catholic hierarchy that he was now ready to restore. The eight apostolic vicars who had governed the eight districts of England were replaced with thirteen diocesan bishops, each with his own see. Wiseman was to become the first Archbishop of Westminster. On 29 September, with the publication of the bull *Universalis Ecclesiae,* the hierarchy was restored and the complex task of restructuring the British Church was given to Wiseman.

Newman had proposed for many years a *via media* that he hoped would reconcile Anglicans and Catholics. With his own conversion he acknowledged that such an endeavour would never work. He was sensitive to the needs of Anglicans who converted and, with this in mind, he composed a short work, *Difficulties felt by Anglicans in submitting to the Catholic Church,* which appeared in 1850. A letter to Lord Fielding on the matter gives an insight into Newman's mind at the time.

'As to this hubbub, I was anxious just at first, when indeed you were here, but I do not see what can come of it, except indeed inconvenience to some individuals, and black looks from friends and strangers.'

The book was, in part, written in the light of his own family experiences. His parents were dead, but his brothers and sisters were largely unsympathetic, if not hostile, to their brother's change of faith. Harriet neither spoke to nor corresponded with Newman from the moment of his conversion to the day of her death, 17 July 1852. She regarded his defection to the loathed Catholic Church as an act of betrayal and was convinced that he would infect her husband with the 'Roman superstition'. Jemima was equally upset, but after an initial silence she maintained a regular and friendly correspondence with her eldest brother, sending pots of marmalade and other small gifts. Charles and Frank had clearly never been fond of their illustrious sibling, and their relationship grew ever more fractious following his conversion and ordination.

There was widespread indignation at what was seen as a papal ploy. The Bishop of London referred to Catholic clergy as 'emissaries of darkness', while the Archbishop of York asserted that 'Rome's ever wakeful ambition is plotting our captivity and ruin'. The Archbishop of Canterbury defined Catholic priests as 'subtle, skilful and insinuating'. The satirical magazine *Punch* published a cartoon in November that year of a masked pontiff laying mitres filled with dynamite in a vault. The caption read: 'The Guy Fawkes of 1850 – preparing to blow up all England!'

Newman House, St Stephen's Green, Dublin. Photo taken by Frank Browne SJ.

CHAPTER 7:
THE CATHOLIC UNIVERSITY

The archbishops and provincial bishops of Ireland met at the Synod of Thurles in mid-August 1850. As part of their administrative deliberations in the wake of Catholic Emancipation, gained in 1829, the bishops agreed to set up a university in Dublin in accordance with an instruction from Pope Pius IX. The principal motive was to provide a Catholic alternative to the education offered by Trinity College, founded in 1594 under Queen Elizabeth I. Since 1637 Catholics had been formally excluded from membership of the college, but with the Catholic Relief Act of 1791 Parliament permitted Catholics access. The bishops were divided over the direction to follow.

In 1845 the British government of Sir Robert Peel had proposed to establish non-denominational colleges in Belfast, Cork and Galway or Limerick. This was a conciliatory move towards Irish Catholics, Presbyterians and other denominations. The Irish bishops wrote to Propaganda Fidei in Rome, asking for advice as to how to proceed. The instruction from Rome was decisive. The 'godless colleges' proposed by the British government had to be opposed at all costs. The congregation directed that the Irish bishops establish a Catholic college along the lines of the venerable University of Louvain in Belgium. The indication was that the college would also serve English, Welsh and Scottish Catholics.

The bishops decided to establish a Catholic University Committee, the most enthusiastic member of which was Dr Paul Cullen, recently returned to Ireland from Rome, after several years as rector of the Pontifical Irish College, to take up the position of Archbishop of Armagh. The Synod of Armagh was

Cullen's first major event and he intended to put his stamp on the Irish bishops. He had represented most of the bishops at the Holy See and had found them a quarrelsome lot. There was a popular saying in Ireland: 'Every parish priest thinks he is the bishop and every bishop thinks he is the pope.'

In July 1851, eleven months after the synod, Cullen visited Newman at the Oratory, inviting him to come to Ireland to assist in the establishment of the university and to become its first rector. Newman deliberated for a while before replying to Cullen. He had first met the Irishman while in Rome and Cullen had acted as an external examiner for Newman's candidate's faculties exam before ordination. The new Oratory at Edgbaston near Birmingham was scarcely three years old and the London Oratory had been established almost at the same time. Neither was without its challenges, but despite Newman's heavy schedule of writing and the teething difficulties of the two Oratories, the invitation was too enticing to refuse. There would be no question of moving definitively to Dublin, but he could not resist the idea of helping found the first Irish Catholic university for the British Isles.

An unexpected event almost put paid to Newman's involvement in the Irish proposal. In the spring and summer of 1851, he gave a series of popular lectures at the Corn Market in Birmingham, which he later published as *The Present Position of Catholics*. During a lecture delivered on 24 July 1850, Newman accused a former Dominican friar, Giacinto Achilli, of being a 'profligate under a cowl ... ravening after sin'. The friar had been imprisoned by the Cardinal Vicar of Rome, but had escaped, and later wrote a book of his exploits during a visit to England. That the former friar had a colourful past, and possibly present, was taken for granted by Protestant readers. Newman unadvisedly hinted at the sexual impropriety of the exuberant Italian and later argued that he had heard about the friar's proclivities from Cardinal Wiseman. Uproar ensued, in some measure prompted by anti-Catholic factions. When he petitioned the Archbishop of Westminster for evidence of Achilli's criminal past, Wiseman proved evasive and claimed he could not recall where the reports had come from. Newman was left to fend for himself. A case was taken by Achilli against Newman, financially supported by various anti-Catholics, which went to trial on 5 November 1851. The speed with which the trial was slated in court, and the fact that the judge was anti-Catholic, alarmed Newman, who began to doubt if he would receive a fair hearing. By coincidence, Newman was appointed by Cullen and the Irish hierarchy as rector of the new university a week later.

In 1852 the Oratory moved from the centre of Birmingham to a poor district largely populated by Irish migrants and this required Newman's attention. Meanwhile, he was trying to work out how to set up the Irish university. He had never been to Ireland and had very few Irish acquaintances. The train and steamboat journeys from Birmingham to Dublin filled him with apprehension.

The first step was to raise awareness of the need for an indigenous university. Both Cullen and Newman agreed that the most efficient way would be through a series of public meetings at which Newman could expound the expediencies and benefits of an indigenous university. On five consecutive Mondays of May and June 1852 the English academic gave lectures in the Pillar Room at the Rotunda on Dublin's Sackville Street.

The lectures, 'The Discourses of the Nature and Scope of University Education in Dublin', later published as *The Idea of a University*, proved immensely popular. Newman explained that his wish was to help the Irish hierarchy to realise Pope Pius's wish for Catholics, who for centuries had been 'insulted, robbed, oppressed and thrust aside'. Irish Catholics usually ended their formal education at seventeen while Irish Protestants continued until they were twenty-one. This clearly gave Protestants a superior education and greater opportunities. He had no need to mention the anti-Catholic bias that excluded the vast majority of the population from high-grade employment.

The universities would not be research facilities, like the academies, but rather places of teaching. Nor would they be formed by the Catholic faith. For Newman, while a religious ethos could underlie the provision of education, the subjects had to be secular and theological, but stand on their merits. Thus medicine, engineering, languages, the sciences and the arts were to be liberal, not bound by any religious restriction. Newman wanted his students to have access to a library that had Catholic literature. By appointing a chaplaincy he wished to ensure that the young students would have a priest who could offer spiritual direction and help them understand the richness of the Catholic faith. He did not envisage education for everyone, for such would be impossible. It was clearly for the elite, where those who studied gained knowledge firstly for themselves and only secondly for the benefit of others.

Newman had probably overestimated the interest of a population emerging from the Irish famine years, which saw a university education, not as a way of developing intellectual talents, but as a means of making money and establishing a career.

On 3 May 1852, following the death of Archbishop Daniel Murray, Cullen was transferred from Armagh to Dublin. While Armagh was the traditional See of St Patrick, the real power and influence lay in Dublin. Newman heard the news with surprise and delight as he foresaw a closer and more intimate relationship with Cullen and his support for the university.

Newman suggested to Cullen that the university should begin modestly and adapt the Oxford model of one-to-one tutorship of students. Cullen agreed in the first instance. He had been Professor of Sacred Scripture and Hebrew at the Pontifical College of Propaganda Fidei in Rome and the two academics had much in common. Newman pointed out that John Leach, Archbishop of Dublin, had attempted to found a university in 1311 or 1312 with the approval of Pope Clement V. The project had never progressed. Perhaps Cullen's energy and vanity would ensure the university finally happened, even if five centuries late.

Newman arrived at the port of Kingstown, south of Dublin, in October 1851 and took up lodgings north of the River Liffey on Dorset Street, close to the Jesuit Church of St Francis Xavier on Gardiner Street. Here he celebrated Mass each morning before crossing the city to St Stephen's Green, which was to be the site of the university. He later moved to Harcourt Street, around the corner from the new premises.

Among the first exigencies in Newman's mind was that of a church, the natural starting point, a *sine qua non*. There were few Catholic churches, as Cullen's parish building programme had not yet got under way. Newman approached the parish priest of nearby St Audoen's, who showed no interest in sharing his church. After further futile attempts to find help from equally unhelpful clergy, Newman decided to build his own church.

Subscriptions, a common source of income at the time, were deemed the most sensible way to raise the necessary capital. The students and tutors could be housed in a number of domestic buildings. Three houses were acquired as halls of residence, University House (or St Patrick's) at 86 St Stephen's Green, St Laurence O'Toole at 16 Harcourt Street, and St Mary's at 6 Harcourt Street. The last was to be the residence of the rector and each house was provided with a reading room, a dining hall and a chapel. On 4 June 1852 Cullen presided at a ceremony during which Newman was installed as pro-rector.

In the same year, Newman received an invitation from Cardinal Wiseman to preach at the celebrations of the restoration of the British hierarchy held in St Mary's College, Oscott. On 13 July he delivered a stirring and evocative sermon, praising the heroes and martyrs of the past and anticipating a glorious future for the Church in the British Isles. The sermon, later widely distributed in pamphlet form, was well received, all the more as it came from the lips of one who had so recently converted to the Catholic faith. The task of the bishops was to help amalgamate the old Catholics, the converts and the waves of migrants, notably from Ireland, who were now arriving in increasing numbers in the wake of the recent famine. What Newman failed to acknowledge was that the Anglican Church commanded the masses and that the revival of reformers such as the Wesley brothers a generation earlier had vastly strengthened Protestantism. Many Anglicans were infuriated that Pope Pius IX had succeeded in restoring the hierarchy and there were riots in some places. An Act of Parliament promulgated in 1851 prohibited Catholic dioceses from using the titles of the Anglican dioceses.

The Achilli trial, which was still ongoing, had been mentally and emotionally exhausting for Newman and, towards the end of 1852, he traveled to Abbotsford, overlooking the River Tweed in Scotland. The house, owned by James Hope Scott, had formerly been the residence of Sir Walter Scott. James and his wife Victoria had been friends of Newman for many years and both were converts. James invited Newman to spend December and January with them. He gratefully accepted the invitation as he felt he would not be welcome to pass Christmas with his sisters or brothers. Lord and Lady Arundel also visited the family for the festive season. Newman wrote several letters to his fellow Oratorians, unable to relax and often engaging in petty issues. A letter to Ambrose St John, written from Abbotsford on 10 January 1853, gives an insight into the difficulties of establishing the Oratory. In it Newman chastises him for various decisions he had taken without asking his permission. He accuses him of trying to run the Oratory without him and concludes that he waited three days before he answered the letter, indicating his profound annoyance. How St John reacted to this shrill letter is unknown. Perhaps silence was the better part. Newman found Abbotsford gloomy and draughty, and was relieved to return to Birmingham before his departure for Ireland in the spring.

The first part of the year was taken up with the Achilli case, which concluded on 25 June, when the jury found Newman guilty of libel. The presiding judge, John Taylor Coleridge, nephew of the poet Samuel Taylor Coleridge, was a founder of the Canterbury Association, which in 1851 had established a colony on South Island in New Zealand under the auspices of the Archbishop of Canterbury. Many members of the Canterbury Association were anti-Catholic in the extreme and the judge did not display impartiality. Newman was aghast at the result as he had steadfastly protested throughout the trial that the charges were based on false allegations.

Coleridge had concluded the trial by declaring that Newman was unable to defend twenty-two of twenty-three acts of slander. Newman had brought some of Achilli's victims from Italy and Malta and intended calling them as witnesses. They had proved expensive guests, and Newman was obliged to pay for their expenses, and those of their husbands. The judge refused to admit their evidence. Newman was found guilty and fined £100. Within days Newman's friends and admirers had raised money to pay the fine and the substantial legal fees, well in excess of £12,000. While Newman was chastened by the trial, his stature rose among many who admired his integrity and deplored the anti-Catholic bias that had led to his condemnation.

One of the first problems Newman faced with regard to the new university was the academic status of the proposed Irish undergraduates. He was taken aback by the poor level of education. Many children had only primary education. The Great Famine (1845–50) had decimated the population and had also left the Irish with a strong anti-British feeling. They blamed the Westminster government for the scarce assistance in their hour of helpless necessity. Pope Pius, by contrast, had organised a collection in 1847 to assist the Irish affected by the potato blight.

A further problem Newman had to face was the dearth of qualified academics who could teach law, letters, science, medicine, theology and philosophy. The founding of new universities throughout Britain offered academics excellent opportunities and it was unreasonable to hope that many would relish the idea of transferring to Ireland. The new university authorities realised that their project would take many years to come to fruition. Newman met several Irish people who explained the struggle of the country to establish some measure of independence from British rule. Daniel O'Connell, the political leader who had campaigned for the rights of Catholics and won emancipation in 1829, had died some years earlier, in 1847. The following year had seen riots across Europe as citizens rebelled against old monarchies. Ireland also had its own rebellious group, the Young Irelanders, who regularly agitated for democratic reform.

Newman had hoped that Cullen's translation to Dublin would facilitate his work and assure him of financial support. He was aware that several rural diocesan bishops viewed him with suspicion, although they were pragmatic. They wanted a good education for the emerging middle-class Catholics, but not an Oxford-style education for an elite, engineered by a recent convert with an English accent. For most Irish bishops, Newman still represented a foreign occupying power. Father Charles Russell of Maynooth College and Father David Moriarty of All Hallows College both warned him that raising money could prove an insurmountable problem. Nonetheless, he travelled around Ireland visiting the bishops and trying to gain their support. He noted in his diary that the bishops seemed to survive on a diet of mutton, which he found indigestible. By contrast, he found extraordinary hospitality from the nuns he visited at their convents.

Cullen, although a supporter of the establishment of the university, adopted an unexpected strategy as he did not want the bishops, whom he intended to unite under his leadership, to suspect that this was his personal project. The bishops would have to support the idea of the university unanimously for it to get off the ground. The Dublin clergy displayed either antipathy or inertia and offered little practical help.

Cullen had gone to Rome as a student at the age of seventeen and had spent the next thirty years of his life in the Eternal

City. He was imbued with *Romanitas*, and could not afford to alienate the Irish bishops. Moreover, he was aware that the hostility engendered by the French Enlightenment was fading. Christianity, in all its branches across Europe, was reasserting itself. Cullen believed that the best way for Ireland to benefit from the renewal was to adapt Roman customs, the way of life to which he had become accustomed. The de facto leader of the Catholic Church in Ireland, through education and active parochial and devotional life, was determined to turn his national flock into active believers united around the person of the supreme pontiff. Newman failed to understand the delicate game Cullen was playing.

During Cullen's reign in Dublin, twenty new parishes were established and he invited over forty religious orders and congregations to establish themselves in the diocese. They ran schools and hospitals, often bolstering up the inadequate resources provided by the British government. Priests dressed in Roman collars and wore the same clerical garb as in Rome. People became used to seeing nuns, religious brothers, priests, monks and friars in a variety of medieval habits not seen in Ireland for centuries. These were designed to attract attention and demonstrate a new, if usually Mediterranean, Church in Ireland.

Cullen's predecessor, Daniel Murray, had opposed the establishment of a university as unrealistic. The other three archbishops of Ireland showed little support – Archbishop John McHale of Tuam actively put obstacles in Newman's way.

There was a further complication that Newman had underestimated. While he was working on the foundation of the university, Cullen was building a diocesan seminary. Although the National Seminary of Maynooth lay within the confines of the diocese, Cullen wanted his own archdiocesan seminary. In 1854 he founded Clonliffe College in Drumcondra, referring to it as 'the apple of his eye'.

Ireland had just struggled through the greatest disaster of the century, the Great Famine, during which over a million people died and a further million emigrated to North and South America and mainland Britain. Nobody could be sure when the blight would return, and those who had lived through the epidemic were little inclined to support a university, which did not figure on their list of priorities.

Tension between Cullen and Newman deepened. Cullen opposed the nationalist Young Irelanders and advised Newman against employing adherents for the new university. To Cullen's chagrin, Newman ignored his advice, countering that these patriots were among the most eligible staff available. Cullen ignored Newman's letters, the tone of which grew increasingly pleading. Cullen may now have regretted the appointment of Newman as rector of the new university and seemed determined to put him in his place.

Nonetheless, the university went ahead. News of Newman's predicament reached the pope's ears. Papal support came in an encyclical published on 23 March 1854, *Optime Noscitis: On the Proposed Catholic University of Ireland*, in which Pius IX expressed frustration at the lethargic support that the bishops had given the project and urged Catholics to offer financial support. 'As We know that you have already chosen Our beloved son, Father John Henry Newman, to govern that university,' wrote Pius, 'We want to approve your choice that this priest, blessed with such wonderful gifts of mind and soul, and endowed with piety, sound doctrine and zeal for the Catholic religion, assume the care and governance of this university and preside over it.' An English chamberlain to Pope Pius, Monsignor George Talbot, wrote to Father Richard Stanton of the London Oratory about how the pope had been influenced by Newman's *Essay on the Development of Doctrine*. According to Talbot, Wiseman and several French bishops attributed the 1854 definition of the dogma of the Immaculate Conception to Newman's theory of the evolution of the teachings of the Church. Although Talbot disliked Newman, he acknowledged that Pius continued to support him.

The new university opened its doors on 3 November with 17 students, including Daniel O'Connell, grandson of the famous politician. Cullen expected Newman to reside in Dublin for the academic year but Newman returned to the Birmingham Oratory regularly to oversee the community and its development as well as purchasing a retreat house at Rednall.

With his conversion, Newman had lost contact with many of his former colleagues. Richard Whately, with whom Newman had been friendly at Oriel College, was appointed by the crown as Archbishop of Dublin in 1831. His official residence was on St Stephen's Green, three minutes' walk from the university. Whately had espoused state support for the Catholic clergy and had proposed the common education of Irish Protestants and Catholics. This was opposed by Cullen and McHale, and Whately gave up the attempt in 1853. Despite their shared interest in education, neither Whately nor Newman met during the latter's time in Dublin.

Newman confided in Wiseman the problems he had with Cullen and the Irish bishops. Wiseman came up with a plan; he would suggest that Pius IX make Newman a bishop. That would give the rector some prestige and help in his dealings with Cullen in particular. When Wiseman suggested this to Pius during an audience, the pope beamed approval. 'We will send him a little cross,' indicating the bishop's pectoral cross, 'and We will make him Bishop of Porfino or somewhere or other.'

In the event, the titular bishopric never materialised. Cullen most probably indicated that he did not want another bishop within his diocese and Wiseman never mentioned it again. When Newman's friend Miss Giberne suggested it to Pius in a private audience one day, the pope 'looked much confused and began to take a great deal of snuff'.

Newman did not know that Pius had vacillated and was convinced that he would become a bishop. On 21 April 1854 Frederick Faber of the London Oratory wrote to Newman with the offer of his confrères and students to pay for the three mitres he would need as a bishop. Newman replied from 16 Harcourt Street in Dublin that he would not like them to incur expense. 'As much love goes with a cheap mitre as a grand one.'

In May that year, Newman wrote to Cullen about committee meetings regarding the university. In the letter he pressed Cullen to ensure that he be appointed Vicar General for the university for a period of three years, citing the lack of interest expressed by several other Irish bishops. 'If they do not,' Newman explained, 'it is very plain I shall not know where I stand.' Cullen ignored the request.

Newman continued his efforts to juggle his commitments with the university and the Oratory. He wrote from Dalkey in south Dublin to a fellow priest, Edward Caswell, at the Oratory, asking him not to interfere with the brothers. A row between Caswell and a Brother Frederic over a perceived insult had boiled over. Newman urged Caswell to leave the brothers to Ambrose St John, who was in charge of them. He also found time to write a novel, *Callista*, set during the early Roman persecutions, which was a veiled attack on the manner in which the British authorities treated Catholics. The novel was published in 1855, the year in which Newman and Faber's disagreements came to a head and when the Oratories of Birmingham and London definitively separated.

Newman shared his frustrations with Elizabeth Bowden in a letter dated 31 August 1855. 'A Rector ought to be a more showy, bustling person than I am ... I ought to dine out every day but of course I don't dine out at all. I ought to mix in literary society and talk about new gasses and the price of labour – whereas I can't remember what I once knew, much less get up a whole lot of new subjects ... and I ought to be above all 20 years younger.'

Newman's frustration with Cullen was evident in a letter to the British MP William Monsell, composed the following month. In the letter he complains of Cullen's lack of communication regarding the granting of degrees in arts. He had called to the archbishop's residence that morning and asked Cullen for an answer. Cullen replied that he could not answer. Newman pressed him again and the archbishop repeated that he could not answer and was going out. Newman related that the meeting lasted scarcely one minute. 'Is there not something of rudeness as regards myself? Might he not have at least said "I will write to Dr Newman"?'

For a man who placed such high regard on writing letters and answering correspondence, Cullen's deliberate silence must have been both discouraging and offensive. Already working with little support from the rural bishops, Newman was increasing isolated as he faced a myriad of administrative problems. Money was not forthcoming, enrolments were low and academic degrees had not been approved by the authorities. Newman wondered who was in charge.

With the Oratory always on his mind, Newman wrote to Wiseman to express his dismay that Propaganda Fidei had changed the rule regarding the care of nuns by the Oratory. Explaining that the change occurred without the Oratorians' knowledge, he asked Wiseman to intervene. While it is unclear whether Wiseman had any knowledge of the move or was involved in it, the issue indicates how Newman perceived Roman interference in the Oratory's affairs. A few weeks later, Newman wrote to Frederick Faber, expressing his annoyance that the London Oratorians had written to Propaganda Fidei for the relaxation of part of the Rule. The Congregation had replied, relaxing the portion also for Birmingham. One of the instances regarded the Oratorians hearing the confessions of nuns. In a long letter, Newman took Faber and his colleagues to task, insisting that he was in charge of all Oratorians in England. The misunderstanding between the two communities brought about a breakdown in relations that led to the London Oratory seeking complete independence.

The rupture in relations between the two Oratories may have been inevitable but also fortuitous. Faber was an able administrator and in 1852 purchased land for a new residence and church in the London suburb of Brompton. Newman had been unhappy with that decision, insisting that St Philip Neri was the apostle of the city and not of the suburbs. However, the new Oratory rapidly gained both a congregation and patrons who helped build the church and residence.

Meanwhile, University Church in Dublin was built quickly and was dedicated to St Peter and St Paul on 1 May 1856. Funds had been slow coming in and public subscriptions had been disappointing. The building of a chapel was not in the original agreement with the Irish bishops but Newman had received a substantial amount of money for the Achilli trial and he donated the residue towards the church campaign. He arranged for the appointment of Father William Anderdon, a former Anglican clergyman, as the chaplain.

Given the location, a neo-Gothic church was out of the question. Moreover, Newman had a particular aversion towards neo-Gothic. Newman invited his friend, John Hungerford Pollen, a former Anglican clergyman who had converted in 1852 and had been appointed Professor of Fine Arts at the university, to design a church vaguely on Byzantine lines. It was built largely in the garden at the rear of one of the university houses. There were no funds for stained glass and the windows were made from the ends of old bottles acquired from the Dublin Glass Bottle Company. Nor was there money for brass candlesticks so wooden bases were used instead. The apse was covered with a canvas that imitated costly mosaic based on the apse of San Clemente in Rome. The hope was, in time, to decorate with real mosaic when funds became available.

Newman did not regard the Catholic University of Ireland as exclusively for the Irish. Writing to Bishop Thomas Grant of Southwark on 7 March 1856, he explained that the university was open to students from the British Isles. However, if a Catholic college were to open in Oxford, he would regard his obligations in Ireland terminated and take up the rectorship of

Oxford. 'If I went by my own wishes, or tendencies, I would far rather do good to English Catholics in Oxford than in Dublin.'

When his contract was terminated Newman may have been relieved to conclude the task that appeared to dwarf him, but he acknowledged that the termination was a rebuff to his professionalism and an unfavourable reflection on his organisational abilities. The failure of the bishops to allow a lay-financial administration and a lay-vice rector rankled in particular. Newman had taken on too many commitments and was unable to fulfil any of them satisfactorily. Over seven years he had made fifty-six crossings to and from Ireland.

The row between the London and Birmingham Oratorians deepened. Newman's weak insistence that he had meant no offence failed to satisfy the London brethren, who wished for complete independence from Newman's control. Newman was annoyed for he believed this lessened his authority as founder of the Oratorians in England. Newman had undertaken a visit to Rome to negotiate the paintings for his university church and, while there, asked for an audience with the pope.

Newman brought Ambrose St John with him for support and for his mastery of Italian. At the end of January, they obtained an hour-long audience with Pope Pius, who received them in his private study. He began by telling Newman that he had lost weight and St John that he had aged since he last saw him. Having talked about various subjects, he abruptly asked what problem they had come to talk about. Newman had spied a letter from the London Oratory on the pope's desk. Pius said he knew all about it but Newman contradicted him. He explained that while the London Oratorians might be disposed to hear nuns' confessions, the Oratorians at Birmingham did not see this as their role. The Oratorian parish had responsibly for a poorhouse, a jail, schools and a hospital. Newman did not want to take on responsibility for hearing nuns' confessions. The pope suggested that a priest might be appointed for that specific purpose but Newman did not see that as a solution.

St John explained that what might suit one Oratory need not suit all. The pope agreed and reiterated that Newman was the apostolic delegate for Oratorians in Britain. Newman was elated with the pope's reaction and a few days later Cardinal Barnabo confirmed that, as papal delegate, Newman had authority over all Oratories in the British Isles. It was to be a pyrrhic victory. Three years later, when his writings were delated to Rome, Cardinal Barnabo sided against him.

The final years in Dublin were increasingly unhappy. Problems at the Oratory and with the English and Irish bishops piled upon him. On 30 October 1856 Newman wrote to St John, explaining his frustration with Frederick Faber, accusing him of jealousy and of stealing Oratorians at Birmingham to set up a rival Oratory in London. 'I go to Rome to be snubbed, I come to Dublin to be repelled by Dr McHale and worn away by Dr Cullen. The Cardinal taunts me with his Dedications and Fr Faber insults me with his letters. And then there is old Talbot, with his platitudes and Fr Dalgairns, scouting my distinct request and going on corresponding with the Fathers.' Comparing himself to Job, he concluded by asking, 'What is to be the end of it?'

In the end, Cullen made it clear that Newman was not carrying out his duties and commitments to the university project and he forced the rector to admit defeat. The archbishop pointed out that in one year there had been only a handful of enrolments. Newman complained about the way the laity had been treated 'like good little boys – told to shut their eyes and open their mouths and take what we give them'. On 12 November Newman resigned as rector of the incipient university and sailed for the last time from Kingstown to England.

With Newman's departure, the university endured several unhappy years until the establishment of the Royal University in 1880, which was open to women. In 1883 Newman's college passed into the care of the Jesuits.

Johann Josef von Döllinger.

CHAPTER 8:
RETURN TO BIRMINGHAM

Back in Birmingham Newman devoted himself to overseeing the Oratory and to a new project that had been suggested to him by the British bishops. In the summer of 1857 Cardinal Wiseman invited Newman to edit a translation of the Bible into English. It was a project to which Newman was well suited. The last great edition of the Bible had been the Douai-Rheims edition published by Bishop Challoner in the seventeenth century. Advances in biblical scholarship and archeological discoveries had changed the world of scriptural studies and Newman would clearly be a good editor and oversee a suitable modern style for the new version. Newman was greatly enthused by the project and set about purchasing books and engaging contributors.

Unluckily for Newman, the American bishops had simultaneously decided to produce a new version known as the Baltimore Bible. Wiseman learned of the American proposal and decided not to go ahead. Inexplicably he did not inform Newman, who continued to work on the project. Only by chance did he learn that his efforts had been in vain, and he faced the embarrassing task of informing the contributors that they would not be needed.

In 1858, Newman heard from his brother Charles, with whom he had last been in contact in 1845. He shared the expense of maintaining Charles with his brother Francis, settling on him an annual income of £70 per annum. Francis was a successful and prodigious author and was generous to Charles. Sixteen years later, Newman wrote that Charles, who lived as a recluse in an attic in Tenby at Carmarthen Bay in Wales, was 'supported almost entirely by the generosity of Frank. He has given up the very thought of me, as if wiped out of the world, since I have become a Catholic.'

In March 1859, Bishop Ullathorne of Birmingham called to the Birmingham Oratory to ask for Newman's assistance with a magazine entitled *The Rambler*. Founded in 1848, the magazine was aimed at an educated lay, consecrated and clerical audience. Topics ranged from history to politics, culture to theology. It followed a broadly liberal line in contrast with the increasingly pro-Roman viewpoint of mid-century Catholicism. Newman was initially reluctant to take on the editorship but, at Ullathorne's persuasion, finally agreed. Newman knew that the editor, Richard Simpson, had been forced out by the bishops for allowing articles critical of Cardinal Wiseman.

The story of *The Rambler* provides a useful key to understanding the state of the Catholic Church in the mid-nineteenth century when two opposing movements formed in the wake of the French Revolution. The Ultramontanists derived their name from the Latin, meaning 'over the mountains', the Alps. The Gallicans referred to the French and, in particular, the liberalising views expressed by the Revolution. The former group counted many converts among their number and both groups were ideologically opposed to each other.

Newman found himself sympathetic to both sides, attracted by the Ultramontanists' devotion to the episcopate and tradition, yet also appreciative of the Gallicans' pragmatic proposal of the need to change and develop. It was typical of Newman's approach of the *via media*. He stuck by the views he expressed in his article but bowed to the pressure of the bishops who had objected and resigned his editorship.

In 1857 several converts to Catholicism had suggested that Newman found a school where members of the Oratory and a lay staff would teach boys. The parents and guardians wanted a Catholic education but they also wanted all the other amenities that the Anglican schools provided. Newman agreed to the idea, despite the opposition of Wiseman. He wrote to Sir John Simeon, another convert, asking for support, proposing to adapt a building in the countryside near the Oratory and take in boys at the age of nine. The appeal for funds was successful, and on 2 May 1859 a small school was formally established at Woodcote near Reading, opening with seven pupils. Newman worried that the London Oratory would also try to open a school in opposition but Faber was unlikely to gain support from the senior Catholic aristocrat, the Duke of Norfolk.

Newman oversaw the purchase and building of the boarding school, ensuring that adequate playing fields were provided and equipping a small theatre where plays and concerts could be performed. A boy's choir would sing at Mass and liturgical ceremonies and a chapel would cater to their religious needs.

As usual, Newman micro-managed the project to the last degree. He ensured that the kitchens provided food that was as nutritious as feasible and he also arranged that the boys had an adequate study hall and supply of books.

All was progressing smoothly for Newman. He always felt that education was his principal gift and he enjoyed the challenge of the new school. Financial support came quickly and the facilities improved.

In July 1859 Newman published an essay, *On Consulting the Faithful in Matters of Doctrine*. The very title alarmed several bishops who saw no place for the laity in the formation of the teaching of the Catholic faith, a task they saw reserved to themselves by virtue of their apostolic office. Then, on 13 January 1860, Bishop Ullathorne informed Newman that the article on consulting the faithful in matters of doctrine had been sent to Rome by an anonymous detractor, later identified as Bishop Thomas Brown of Newport and Menevia, and that Propaganda Fidei would investigate its orthodoxy.

Newman was taken aback and expressed his irritation to a friend. The idea of being summoned to Rome to answer complex theological arguments with an Italian was preposterous. Of particular worry was that rumours of his delation to Rome quickly spread among the parents of the Oratory School pupils and enrolments were adversely affected. In a letter to Ambrose St John in 1860 Newman vented his frustration.

'When I was 20 I was cut off from the rising talent of the University by my failure in the Schools, as, when 30, I was cut off from distinction in the governing body by being deprived of my Tutorship, as when 40 I was virtually cast out of the Church of England, by the affair of No. 90, as when 50 I was cast out of what may be called society by the disgrace of the Achilli sentence, so when I should arrive at 60 years, I should be cast out of the good books of Catholics, and especially of ecclesiastical authorities ... this appals me in this way – viz, what is to happen, if I live to be seventy?' Newman hoped that his closest friend would offer some comforting response to these rhetorical questions. Newman's theology, with his Anglican heritage, was more advanced than that of the Catholic bishops. Now most of the bishops turned against him and even Pope Pius began to have doubts.

The new school suddenly experienced a number of difficulties. Newman had experience with mature students but none with very young children. The headmaster, Father Nicholas Darnell, proved ill-suited to the school wished for by the Oratorians and, after several rows, resigned along with the rest of the teaching staff. Newman entreated him unsuccessfully to return and was forced to appoint Ambrose St John as a temporary principal. While he slowly won the support of the parents, he found the strain almost intolerable.

In 1860 Newman's fellow convert and Oratorian, Frederick Bowles, left the Oratorians for diocesan priesthood. Two years later, John Flanagan, who had joined the Oratory in 1848, returned to Ireland. Newman wrote of the period in his autobiography, 'As a Protestant, I felt my religion dreary, but not my life – but, as a Catholic, my life dreary, not my religion.'

Although he had severed his ties with Oxford and was deeply

saddened by his self-imposed exile from his intellectual alma mater, Newman hoped to set up an Oratory there. He believed that it would be of use to young Catholics studying in Oxford. 'I would rather have Catholic youths in Protestant Colleges in Oxford with a strong Catholic Mission in the place than a Catholic College.'

In 1864, Newman was contacted by a man who had recently purchased five acres in central Oxford, which he offered to sell for £8,000. Newman was willing to purchase the land and, at Bishop Ullathorne's suggestion, contemplated opening an Oratory there.

At this point, Rome interfered, probably at the prompting of Cardinal Wiseman. Newman's reluctance to foster conversions had surprised Wiseman. At his suggestion, the bishops met officials at Propaganda Fidei in Rome. The decision was made by the English bishops and Roman officials not to progress with a Catholic college at Oxford. Some time later Cardinal Bembo, Prefect of the Congregation for Propaganda Fidei, wrote a condescending letter to Newman, explaining that the decision was due to 'the recent unhappy perversion of a number of Catholic youths'.

Newman had faced many disappointments in the two decades since his conversion. A failed university, an abandoned plan to translate the Bible, a brief effort to edit a Catholic magazine; none of these amounted to anything of which to be proud. Perhaps in old age he reflected on the failures and saw that they spurred him on to greater achievements. Throughout his life, Newman reacted to situations. He was not an innovator but his temperament allowed him to absorb vast amounts of pertinent material, reflect maturely and then lay out his response in carefully reasoned essays and books.

Writing some years later, Newman related how a general malaise had overtaken him. He was lethargic and depressed. Shortly before his sixty-fifth birthday he thought about his impending death. By the standards of the day he was a relatively old man and he began make preparations for his death and his succession at the Oratory.

Throughout this time Newman continued to follow theological developments across Europe. In August 1863, the Munich Conference took place in Bavaria, chaired by his friend Döllinger. The conference attempted to infuse Catholicism with enthusiasm for ecumenical unity and Newman was well placed to understand that. Döllinger urged theologians not to confine themselves to the scholasticism proposed by the medieval Dominican theologian, St Thomas Aquinas, and, moreover, to accept that many of the Reformed Churches had important contributions to make to the Catholic Church. While Pope Pius IX had sent a blessing in advance of the meeting, he was disturbed by the reports sent to Rome. The Roman Curia was more interested in preserving the role of the Petrine office than exploring new alliances with schismatic churches. Newman, however, read with interest the proceedings of the gathering and found himself in broad agreement with the premise that Catholic theologians should study the early Church Fathers.

In England, *The Home and Foreign Review*, published by John Acton and with Newman's support, published an article praising the work of Döllinger. However, on 21 December 1863 Pius IX sent a letter to the Archbishop of Munich insisting that the Church continue to favour medieval theology and that the German theologians must submit to papal authority in all matters.

English Protestants saw in this reaction a further example of the narrow-minded viewpoint of Rome. Newman agreed, blaming Propaganda Fidei for shaping the pope's view. When Acton published the final edition of the paper in April 1864, Newman wrote a letter of support and resolved not to write on these issues again.

Febr. 27. 1885

My dear Fr Hopkins

Thank you
for your very kind remembrance
of my birthday I am so sorry to
to say my hand is too weak now to
enable me to write — and I fear the
weakness is permanent. I grieve to
find you corroborate from your own experience what other friends tell me about
the state of Ireland. What are we coming to!

Yours affecty S H Card. Newman

Letter from Newman to Gerard Manley Hopkins SJ,
dated 27 February 1885.

CHAPTER 9: APOLOGIAE

Basically conservative and pro empire, he [Gerard Manley Hopkins] worried about the empire's possible fragmentation under Gladstone and did not favour the repeal of the Act of Union. However, attentive always to suffering of any kind, he did not deny that Ireland was neglected and mismanaged by Britain.

Writing of these concerns to his mentor, Blessed J. H. Newman, the latter's pointed reply [letter above dated 3 March 1887] must have rocked the poet: 'If I were an Irishman, I should be [in heart] a rebel'.

(From Introduction to the Dark Sonnets, *Bright Wings, Dappled Things*, Messenger Publications 2018, p.91)

A mundane insult stirred Newman to compose his best-known work. In December 1863, the Regius Professor of Cambridge University and tutor to the Prince of Wales published an anonymous article in *Macmillan's Magazine* in which he accused the Catholic clergy, and John Henry Newman in particular, of not regarding truth as a virtue. At first glance, the article was polemical and not worthy of a riposte. Newman contacted the editors to inquire as to the identity of the author and to insist on a retraction of the slander. Charles Kingsley revealed his authorship in a pamphlet entitled *What then does Dr. Newman mean?*, in which he accused Newman of dishonesty. 'Truth, for its own sake, has never been a virtue with the Roman Catholic clergy. Father Newman informs us that it need not be, and, on the whole, ought not be.'

Newman was pricked by the insult, not so much to his good name but to his reputation as an honest and truthful person. He realised also that any offence to him or his integrity would reflect negatively on other converts and his Oratorians. At first he sought to ignore the slight, but as he thought more about it, he realised that it could not go unchallenged.

Kingsley was a clergyman, Regius Professor of Modern History at Cambridge, prolific writer of novels, sermons and treatises and a friend and supporter of the botanist Charles Darwin, whom Newman admired and whose work he had read. Kingsley was a respected writer and his novel *The Water Babies* would become a timeless classic.

At the basis of Kingsley's diatribe was the allegation that Newman had never been a true Anglican but a Catholic in disguise. This made no sense because Newman had been raised within the Church of England, with Calvinist leanings imbibed from his mother. Although the charge was merely provocative, Newman rose to the challenge.

In his finished work, *Apologia Pro Vita Sua*, Newman sought not to apologise for his faith but to explain how he had always acted with integrity. He noted that, upon reading Kingsley's attack, within half an hour he decided to counter the attack, not so much to defend his name as the integrity of the Catholic priesthood.

In the opening of his work, published in instalments, Newman thanked Kingsley for granting him the opportunity of reflecting on his life and enumerating the events and works that formed it. He then accused him of dishonesty. The work was a masterpiece of understatement, as Newman pretended that he must have misunderstood Kingsley, for nobody could be as 'silly' as to say the things that appeared to have been written. Having hoisted Kingsley on his own petard, Newman proceeded to expose him as a 'knave'. Despite all his learning, Kingsley was narrow-minded and a racist. Newman cunningly protested that he wrote to defend the Catholic priesthood but he laid bare Kingsley's bias and lack of logic. From there he gave an account of the salient events and writings of his life.

The book was widely read by Anglicans and Catholics as well as believers in other faiths. To his pleasure, Newman found the response overwhelmingly positive and, to the publisher's delight, the book sold extremely well. Newman was particularly pleased to receive letters from former acquaintances and friends from whom he had been estranged. Among the letters was one from a former parishioner, Charles Crawley, a retired merchant who had greatly admired the vicar but had not understood the reasons for his conversion. Another welcome reconnection came when his old friend and fellow tutor, Richard Church, Dean of St Paul's in London, made contact and the two men took up a pleasant correspondence that lasted until Newman's death.

Newman had increasingly influenced converts to Catholicism, and had kept up faithful correspondence with a large number of friends, acquaintances and strangers. He simultaneously began new dialogues with curious Anglicans. In 1866 he received Gerald Manley Hopkins into the Catholic Church and, the following year, arranged for him to teach at the Oratory School. The young academic, who had taken a double first at Oxford, remained at the Oratory until he left to join the Jesuits in 1868, although Newman continued to correspond with him.

Newman, true to his Evangelical background, never expressed a strong devotion to the figure of Mary, mother of Jesus. He shared the Anglican view that an exaggerated form of Marian piety was almost idolatrous. In dialogue with Edward Pusey in 1866, he examined the figure of Mary in the New Testament and the writings of the early Church Fathers, and wrote a series of meditations on her role in salvation history. Many Anglicans were interested in the scriptural and patristical basis of Newman's scholarship. It proved a link in the improving relations between some Anglicans. In his poem 'The Dream of Gerontius', published in 1865, Newman explored the concept of Purgatory, important in Catholicism but rejected by Luther and the reformers of the sixteenth century. The deathbed confession of Gerontius proved popular with Victorian audiences as it explored the theme of Purgatory.

With the death of Nicholas Wiseman in 1865, the most important diocese in England became vacant. Newman and the Oratorians also lost a patron. Pope Pius decided, against the advice of his counsellors, to appoint Henry Manning, who had been ordained by Wiseman ten weeks after his conversion in 1851. Apart from his personal appreciation of Manning, Pius may have hoped that the appointment to London of a high-profile convert and former Anglican clergyman would have a substantial impact on Victorian society. Newman was wary of Manning and of the latter's keen sense of authority. Although a convert, Manning appreciated the complexity of the Catholic clerical world and its hierarchy. Newman was an idealist while Manning was a pragmatist. While Newman teased out the idea that Christian belief grows slowly, Manning seemed to believe that everything one needed to know was in the Bible and the catechism. On more than one occasion Newman confided to his friends that Manning had never truly become a Catholic but had remained an Anglican at heart. It was an unfair assessment as Manning proved to be a highly competent and successful Archbishop of Westminster.

Newman continued to follow the lives of all his friends through his regular letters. One of his bitterest bereavements came in late 1867 with the news of the death of a Visitation nun, Sister Dominica Bowden, the daughter of his close friend from Oxford days, John Bowden. Newman had baptised Marianne in 1831, had encouraged her conversion in 1847 and had preached at the Mass during which she had taken her final vows. Over the years the two had kept up an affectionate correspondence. Only Newman's letters survive. He confided his financial worries as well as his frustrations to her. He wrote about pleasant day trips to the seaside and grumbled about growing old. He shared his plans to open an Oratory at Oxford and the way in which the bishops thwarted his intentions. He treasured her evident kindness and encouragement. When she died, Newman wrote of his distress to the mother superior of the convent in Sussex. 'I was not prepared for your letter. She was young and I am old and she is taken before me. May I follow her and my soul be with hers!'

Whereas Newman normally wrote for publication in response to an issue of the day or to an attack, his longest book took twenty years to write and was on a general theme. He was a seasoned writer and wrote rapidly. His brother Oratorians, notably Ambrose St John and Newman's secretary William Payne Neville, would regularly spend hours transcribing pages with passages crossed out and rewritten into fair copies ready for publication. Even with the introduction of typewriters in the

1880s Newman continued to write by hand, using a sharpened feather quill or metal nib. *The Grammar of Assent,* published in 1870, stands out in Newman's writings as it does not simply deal with the theology and traditions of the Christian Churches but rather the relationship of faith and reason.

Newman had long been fascinated by the writings of the British empiricists such as Hume, Lock and Stuart Mill. Although he did not profess to be a philosopher but rather a theologian, he understood that while not everybody was interested in theology, everybody was, whether they knew it or not, interested in philosophy. Newman tackled the subject of faith and reason at the suggestion of his friend W. G. Ward. While travelling in Switzerland with Ambrose St John in August 1864, Newman had a moment of inspiration. He wished to explore how everybody could grasp the truths of Christianity without being able logically to explain the basis of their faith. He spent a few days teasing out the idea at Lake Geneva. The idea had simmered in his mind for several years and now he found answers to questions for which he had long searched. He was aware that many in Britain belonged to the Anglican Church but had little personal faith in God, made manifest in the person of Jesus. He wanted to reach out to those and stimulate their religious imagination.

In 1874 a further controversy provoked Newman's intervention, the reply to an apparently innocuous remark by a former prime minister.

William Gladstone entered the House of Commons in 1832 and served under Sir Robert Peel. He was a founding member of the Conservative Party in 1834 and joined the Liberal Party in 1859. He was first appointed British prime minister in 1868 and held the premiership until his electoral defeat in 1874 when he resigned as leader of the Liberal Party.

Gladstone, a baptised Anglican, shared the vague anti-Catholic bias of the age. He argued that as the Anglican Church was established as the state Church and protected by the crown, it should not pay money to other Christian denominations. In 1845, when Sir Robert Peel proposed increasing the annual grant to the Irish seminary of St Patrick's College in Maynooth, County Kildare, Gladstone protested that such a move was against the wishes of the crown. When Peel's government fell the following year, Gladstone was elected to represent the University of Oxford at Parliament, and he served as chancellor of the exchequer from 1859 to 1866.

In October 1874, Gladstone published an article in the *Contemporary Review* dealing with the role of ritual in the Church of England. In passing, he stated that nobody could convert to Catholicism without losing his moral and mental freedom and still remain a loyal citizen.

Such a remark would probably have gone largely unnoticed had Gladstone not repeated and expanded his views the following month in a tract entitled *The Vatican Decrees and their Bearing on Civil Allegiance*. The reaction was explosive. Gladstone was accusing Catholics of disloyalty to the British crown, effectively branding them traitors. Neither cradle Catholics nor converts could be expected to take this libellous charge without a riposte.

Gladstone was a politician with no theological training. He confused the recently promulgated dogma of papal infallibility with an oath of civic loyalty. Many protested to him both privately and publicly. The Marquis of Ripon, a recent convert to Catholicism, wrote to Gladstone, pointing out that Catholics were no less loyal than any other English citizen by virtue of their faith. Gladstone privately agreed with Ripon, yet in public he continued to argue Catholic disloyalty in a short work, *Vaticanism*, published in February 1875.

The success of his *Apologia Pro Vita Sua* had both sharpened Newman's skill as an apologist, or defender, of the Catholic faith, and had given him an international profile. Many English Catholics now looked to Newman as much as to their bishops for intellectual leadership. It came as no surprise when he emerged to challenge Gladstone's arguments. A large number of Catholics had appealed to Newman, knowing that he was the best placed to take on the former prime minister, given that Newman and Gladstone had many friends in common. He needed little encouragement, for he was indignant at Gladstone's ignorance and desirous of defending the truth, as he saw it.

The riposte to Gladstone came in the form of a lengthy letter addressed to the Duke of Norfolk, the premier Catholic aristocrat in Great Britain. The tone was notably reserved. Unlike in the *Apologia*, Newman confined his counter-arguments to theology and, mining voluminous quotations from centuries of the Christian tradition, undermined Gladstone's thesis. He did not seek to humiliate Gladstone for his lack of theological preparation or knowledge of ecclesiastical history, but chose to see the best in what Gladstone had written. In reality, Gladstone's premise was unsustainable. Newman used Gladstone's protestations to build a clear delineation of papal authority in matters of morality and doctrine, but agreed that in all other matters the pope could err like any other human. The *Letter to the Duke* clarified for many Catholic teaching on conscience.

The Duke of Norfolk had only reluctantly agreed to the dedication of the book. The English bishops, apart from Archbishop Manning, remained noticeably quiet in the verbal affray. Had Newman written such a work prior to the convocation of the First Vatican Council, it is possible that the issue of infallibility may have been addressed differently and a more nuanced definition achieved. In truth, Gladstone was not particularly interested in the indignation of many Catholics.

Throughout the course of his pontificate, Pius IX had become increasingly conservative in political and theological matters. He had good reason to be concerned over the political fate of the Italian peninsula. Since the Middle Ages Italy had been divided into duchies, republics and city states. The second half of the nineteenth century had seen an increasing move towards unification as a kingdom. Many had initially hoped that Pius might be the first king, but that aspiration had died after the revolution of 1848.

Since the eighth century the popes had controlled a vast swathe of land, the Papal States, which ran roughly from Rome in the west to the Marches in the north-east. By 1861 much of these territories had come under the control of the Kingdom of Italy. As the pope's temporal power was eroded, he sought to elevate his spiritual power.

In the early 1860s, Pope Pius decided to convoke an ecumenical council. Such global meetings of the world's bishops were rare, only nineteen having taken place in the previous nineteen centuries. The Council of Trent, called to face the challenge of the Protestant Reformation, had closed three centuries earlier in 1563.

Ecumenical councils are generally convened in response to a particular problem. The Catholic Church was still trying to come to terms with the upheaval caused by the Age of Enlightenment and the French Revolution in the eighteenth century, and the recent national rebellions in various European nations in the nineteenth. Pius and his advisers intended that such a gathering would present an unequivocal response to the liberalism and rationalism that had grown in political and Church circles. Throughout the nineteenth century advances in anthropology, science, archaeology and geology left many Christians dismayed as previous certainties were undermined.

During the years of preparation from 1864 to the opening of the council on 8 December 1869, bishops invited theologians to assist them in the contributions to debates. Although Newman was not invited to the council as a theological expert, several bishops were influenced by his outlining of the unbroken line of tradition by tracing all teachings to the apostolic era.

The council was short-lived. The first constitution, *Dei Filius,* on the nature of the Catholic faith, passed unanimously on 24 April 1870. The second constitution, *Pastor Aeternus,* dealt with the nature of the Church. Controversially, the question of papal infallibility, the obligation of the pope to speak in a binding manner on matters of faith and morals, was raised. There was intense opposition to the wisdom of defining infallibility, but the majority of the bishops, at the insistence of the pope, voted in favour of doing so.

The concept of papal infallibility concerns the role of the pope as steward of the Catholic faith. The First Vatican Council defined the dogma as the obligation of the pope to clarify aspects of Catholic theology and morality in accordance with the apostolic tradition, which has been taught from the earliest times and has been agreed everywhere. The pope, as successor of St Peter, speaks *ex cathedra*, literally, from the chair, in union with the bishops of the world. In speaking authoritatively, the pope is preserved from teaching heresy or error.

The outbreak of the Franco-Prussian War on 19 July 1870 led to the suspension of the council and the bishops quickly dispersed to their home countries. Piedmontese troops entered Rome on 20 September and occupied the city. The intention was to reconvene the council when the city had been liberated, but on 20 October Pius suspended the gathering indefinitely. A plebiscite decided to end the Papal States and Rome became the capital of the new Kingdom of Italy. The council had begun by examining the role of bishops. By its suspension it shaped Catholic theology for the next eighty years.

Newman followed the reports of the council in the newspapers and in the Catholic press. He expected that the council would continue when the political situation had settled, but even before it had begun he expressed his doubts in a letter to Ambrose St John. 'We must hope, for one is obliged to hope it, that the pope will be driven from Rome, and will not continue the Council or there will be another pope. It is sad that he should force us to such wishes.'

In the event, Newman partially got his wish. The pope was not driven from Rome nor did he die. With the establishment of the Kingdom of Italy, Pius withdrew from his residence at the

Quirinal to the Apostolic Palace beside St Peter's Basilica, where he ended his days as 'a prisoner of the Vatican'.

'We have come to a climax of tyranny,' Newman reflected. 'It is not good for a pope to live twenty years. It is anomaly and bears no good fruit; he becomes a god, has nobody to contradict him, does not know the facts, and does cruel things without meaning it.' There was no personal animosity against Pius, from whom he had received extraordinary respect and support. Papal abdications were rare and Newman's concern was the length of some pontificates, several of which ended in ignominy or senility.

When Pius IX died on February 1878, he had the sympathy of Catholics throughout the world, although the political influence of the papacy had declined across Europe. Newman, unaware how ambivalent Pius had been in his regard, mourned the loss of his great patron who had smoothed his path to the priesthood.

CHAPTER 10:
CARDINAL NEWMAN

From right to left: Father Thomas Pope, Father William Neville,
Father Paul Eaglesim, Cardinal Newman, the Cardinal's 'Gentiluomo',
the 'Caudatario', or Trainbearer. May 1879.

In May 1875, Newman lost his closest friend and confidant of thirty-two years. The previous month Ambrose St John had walked to the house of the Passionist Congregation two miles away for a High Mass. He had suffered a stroke and was semi-paralysed. He made a very slow recovery but by mid-May the doctor told his confrères that he appeared to be out of danger and would further improve. Newman later wrote of the 'jubilation' he felt because his friend was recovering. He bitterly reproached himself for overloading St John with work and felt that this had brought on the stroke.

On the evening of 24 May Newman visited St John in his room. He was taken aback as his friend, unable to speak, embraced him. Shortly before midnight he took a turn for the worse. The brother who was nursing him sent word to Newman but he arrived shortly after his friend had died. He was inconsolable and wept uncontrollably, throwing himself on the bed. Despite the late hour he celebrated a Requiem Mass and immediately wrote to tell St John's family.

Newman received enormous numbers of letters of sympathy. Replying to one he wrote, 'I have ever thought that no bereavement was equal to that of a husband's or a wife's, but I feel it difficult to believe that any can be greater, or anyone's sorrow greater than mine.' It reflected an earlier expression of their relationship. 'From the first he loved me with an intensity of love which was unaccountable. At Rome 28 years ago he was always so working for and relieving me of all trouble, that being young and Saxon-looking, the Romans called him my Guardian Angel. As far as this world is concerned, I was his first and his last.'

That same month, Newman made a long-delayed return to Oxford. Thirty years had elapsed since his departure from his beloved city and the course of his life had changed dramatically. Anti-Catholicism had waned to a degree. The reason for his return was an invitation from Trinity College, his alma mater, which had decided to grant him the first honorary fellowship in 1877. He made the emotional return to Oxford for the ceremony, pausing in Littlemore for a few hours and visiting his old friend John Keble. Two years earlier, in 1876, Newman had asked Anne Mozley, his two sisters' sister-in-law, to edit his letters prior to his conversion. Although Anne was Anglican, she was fond of Newman and readily undertook the task. Newman spent the two subsequent years preparing the letters. He wrote, 'When I have a little leisure, I recur to my pigeon-hole of letters … I do a little work in sifting, sorting, preserving or burning.' Newman may have suspected that interest would continue even after his death. He was determined to be his own editor and decide what should last and what should be destroyed.

The election of the sixty-seven-year-old Gioacchino Pecci as Leo XIII on 20 February 1878 marked a cautious rapprochement with the Italian state. Pecci, a former papal diplomat, had represented the Holy See in Belgium as papal nuncio and had formed close alliances with the aristocracy. At a court dinner he was placed beside his former colleague, the Anglican Archbishop of Dublin, Richard Whately. The conversation turned to the Oxford Movement and the developments in the churches. Whately reminisced about his Oxford days, and recounted some anecdotes of his friend Newman, whom Pecci said he admired.

Pecci visited London, where he was presented to Queen Victoria. He spent some weeks with Cardinal Wiseman and became familiar with the ecclesiastical situation in England. As pope, Leo distanced himself from Pius's isolationist politics. He had long been a supporter of university education and, although theologically conservative, supported the Belgian

University of Louvain at its foundation. In the year before his election, Pecci had published a pastoral letter underlining the harmony between the Church and civilisation.

As he entered his eightieth year, Newman was to receive an entirely unexpected honour. The suggestion to include Newman in Leo's first consistory of ten new cardinals came from the Duke of Norfolk, the duke's cousin, Cardinal Howard, and several lay Catholics. The duke had been a pupil at the Birmingham Oratory School between 1861 and 1864 and greatly admired Newman. In the summer of 1878, the Duke of Norfolk and the Marquis of Ripon approached Cardinal Manning to make the suggestion. Cardinal Howard offered to bring a letter from Manning to Rome and present it personally to the pope. However, as Howard had still not seen Pope Leo by December, the duke took advantage of a visit to Rome to petition the pope personally at the Vatican.

There is no record of Manning's view on Newman's elevation. The two men, although both high-profile converts, were very different from each other. Newman lived a largely secluded life in Birmingham while Manning administered the metropolis of London. Newman's interests were intellectual and literary. Manning worked hard for impoverished Irish immigrants and on behalf of the poor Catholics of the diocese. While he may have preferred to remain the only resident English cardinal, the elderly Newman posed little threat to his place in the hierarchy.

In January 1879, rumours began to reach Newman at the Birmingham Oratory that Pope Leo XIII intended to create him a cardinal. The principal task of the 'Princes of the Church' was to elect a pope, but the position was considered to be an honour. There were various dioceses across the globe where the archbishop of an important city was named a cardinal. The remainder resided in Rome, usually as prefects of various Vatican departments.

Newman was alarmed as he was already in his eightieth year, and he felt the time for such an honour long past. In response to the letters of congratulations that began to arrive, he lamented that he was old and could not be expected to live in Rome, surrounded by people who did not speak his language. He knew, moreover, that he had enemies who were irritated that he had not supported the decree on papal supremacy at the First Vatican Council. What would they do now if he arrived to take up residence in the Eternal City?

While the elderly Oratorian may have been concerned at the threatened upheaval if he should accept the cardinal's hat, he saw the proposal as a vindication of his theological journey and the vanquishing of several enemies. Chief among these were Monsignor George Talbot, with whom Newman had had several disagreements. Talbot, the fifth son of the Baron of Malahide in Dublin, had studied at Oxford and had been ordained an Anglican clergyman. He was received into the Catholic Church by Wiseman in 1842 and was ordained four years later. In 1847 he applied to join Newman's English Oratory, a request that Newman refused. Through Wiseman's influence Talbot went to Rome where he found a position as a papal chamberlain at the court of Pius IX. Talbot disliked Newman intensely and tried to influence Pius against the illustrious convert. However, with a new pope, the old courtiers were gone and Leo's allies took their place.

Newman need not have worried as the pope had decided to dispense with the requirement of residence in Rome. Leo was in the process of dismantling some of the Roman court that had surrounded his predecessor. He was more concerned with finding a political accommodation of the Church and European states than theology. By appointing Newman with the honorific title, he intended to send a signal of his approval and appreciation of the peculiar blend of independence and fidelity that Newman had shown. At Newman's request, Pope Leo agreed not to insist on episcopal consecration, by then the norm for cardinals.

Accompanied by his secretary, Fr Richard Neville, Newman travelled from Birmingham to London on 16 April 1879, and the following day went by train to Folkestone, before journeying onwards via Paris, across the Alps and down through Italy, staying at Turin, Genoa, Pisa and Siena, arriving in Rome within ten days. On the morning of 27 April, Pope Leo XIII received the cardinal-elect in private audience at the Apostolic Palace. During the audience, Newman thanked the pope and expressed his wonder at the papal honour. Leo explained that apart from his desire to pay tribute to Newman and his life's work, the gesture was also designed to give honour to England and the Catholic community, which had experienced considerable growth. To another visitor Leo confided, 'My cardinal ... it was not easy, they saying he was too liberal, but I had determined in honouring the Church in honouring Newman. I had always a cult for him.'

On Monday morning, 12 May, the cardinal-designate went to the Palazzo della Pigna close to the Pantheon. Cardinal Howard had an apartment in the sixteenth-century building and invited Newman and his friends to await the arrival of the pope's chamberlain with a letter from the Cardinal Secretary of State.

Among the dignitaries gathered in the large salon were many English and Irish people living in Rome. Shortly after midday, the chamberlain arrived and was accompanied to the upper floor where Newman was seated. Genuflecting before the Englishman, the chamberlain offered the envelope bearing the seal of Cardinal Antonelli. Newman opened the envelope and read the letter, the contents of which he knew already. Cardinal Antonelli, Secretary of State, informed the English cleric that at a consistory held earlier that morning, Pope Leo XIII had decided to raise Newman to the dignity of the cardinalate and make him a member of the Sacred College of Cardinals, assigning him the titular church of San Giorgio in Velabro, close to the Circus Maximus.

In former years, the arrival of the *biglietto* was something of a staged surprise, and the candidate was expected to express astonishment at the unexpected news and profess his unworthiness of such an honour. The Italians had perfected this to a most refined art, swooning and fainting at the greatness thrust upon their unworthy shoulders. In more recent years, the ceremony had become more formal and the candidate was expected simply to defer to the pope's will and convey his grateful thanks to the sovereign pontiff.

It would have been impossible for Newman to pass up an opportunity to speak and so he produced a few sheets on which he had written out a lengthy address. He began by offering his gratitude to Pope Leo XIII. Acknowledging that the honour was for English Catholics and Protestants, Newman asserted that throughout the course of his life he had tried to oppose Liberalism. By this he meant a tendency to view everything in a relative manner. Such an approach meant that there was no objective truth and that everything was simply subjective or relative. This was an error in Newman's view, in particular in the area of religion, where all were seen as equally valid. Religion is restricted to the private sphere and is excluded from society. In particular, Newman noted, 'everywhere that goodly framework of society, which is the creation of Christianity, is throwing off Christianity.' While Christianity had contributed a vast amount to the formation of society, 'now philosophers and politicians are bent on satisfying this problem without the aid of Christianity.' He concluded that Christianity had survived many persecutions in the past and therefore should continue to hope in God. 'Christianity has too often been in what seemed deadly peril that we should fear for it in any new trial now.' No English bishops were present as they were meeting in London. Cardinal Manning dispatched a formal letter of congratulations, notable only for its lack of warmth.

On 15 May the pope held a public consistory at which he conferred the *galero*, the broad-brimmed tasselled hat that would also be used in Newman's coat of arms, the motto of which read *cor ad cor loquitur* – heart speaks to heart. The English cardinal had adapted this from the writings of the

French bishop, St Francis de Sales. As part of the honours, Newman was appointed a consultor to the Congregations of the Propagation of the Faith (Propaganda Fidei), of Catholic Instruction and of Indulgence and Relics.

Three days after the public ceremonies were concluded, Newman collapsed from exhaustion and remained in seclusion until the end of the month, forgoing the *visite di calore*, when well-wishers could call on the new cardinal. The journey to Rome and the various receptions had been draining and Newman delayed his return to England until midsummer. Upon his return he chose not to have a public reception in his honour but celebrated with a dinner with his confrères.

The reception Cardinal Newman received was extraordinarily warm. There were many invitations throughout the year. As Newman wanted to attend as many events as possible, his secretary extended these into the following year. To mark the first anniversary of the honour, Cardinal Newman travelled to London to stay at the city home of the Duke of Norfolk for a few days filled with receptions and luncheons. The cardinal visited the London Oratory where he gave Benediction.

He returned to his beloved Oxford on Saturday, 22 May, to Trinity College, where a welcome ceremony had been organised, at which an address delicately recorded his scholarly achievements. He preached twice at St Aloysius, the parish administered by the Jesuits.

While many expected the cardinal to retire, Newman now made his last literary foray, as usual to defend his reputation or the Catholic faith. An exchange of correspondence between Gladstone and Newman sparked off the final literary debate. In December 1881 Gladstone wrote to Newman from Hawarden Castle near Chester, expressing his concern over the situation in Ireland. Rebellion was in the air and the British government was unable to pacify those who agitated for independence. Gladstone made no reference to the historical abuse of centuries of occupation and exploitation. Instead he recalled that in

1844, when his government was dealing with 'manifestations' by Daniel O'Connell, an appeal was made to Pope Gregory XIV to intervene. Gladstone enclosed some sermons from Catholic clergy in Ireland which he thought were seditious; had these been laymen, he argued, they could have been put in jail. If these men had contested the decrees of the Council of 1870, Gladstone claimed, surely they would have been silenced. Could the pope not now censure them for, if so, peace could be more easily achieved?

Newman replied from Birmingham on 23 December that Gladstone underestimated the limits of the Petrine office. 'I think you overrate the Pope's power in political and social matters. It is absolute in questions of authority, but not so in practical matters.' He went on to recall how Pope Pius IX, when encouraging him to found an Oratory in England, gave him an Oratory church and library in Malta where the community had died out. Newman had evidently considered the papal gift and may have been tempted to accept it until a friend warned him, 'The Pope is of course acting within his right, but don't fancy you have the House because he has given it. Everything will depend on the Bishop at Malta. Do you know *him?*'

Thus Newman amicably explained that the pope's role is much exaggerated and misunderstood. He concluded by stating the principle of subsidiarity. 'I observe that your letters relate mainly to the intemperate, dangerous words of Priests and Curates. Surely such persons belong to their respective bishops, and scarcely require the intervention of the Supreme Authority?'

To Newman's sorrow, his sister Jemima had died in 1881, and on 22 March 1884, Charles Newman died at Tenby in Wales. Newman had travelled to see his eccentric brother two years earlier but when he arrived at his lodgings, Charles refused to let him in. Newman had been obliged to make the return journey without glimpsing or speaking with his estranged sibling. Upon hearing of his brother's demise, John Henry paid

for the funeral expenses in Tenby and later paid for the erection
of the headstone on which was carved

Domine Misericordia Tua in Saecula
Opera Manuum Tuarum Ne Dispicias
Lord, your mercy lasts forever,
discard not the work of your hands.

CHAPTER 11:
NEWMAN'S LAST YEARS

The last decade of Newman's life was relatively tranquil. His publications largely ceased, apart from a revision of a life of Athanasius in 1886 and a response to an academic. He lived at the Oratory in Edgbaston and rarely attended public functions. He was happiest in his room where he read, seated in a leather armchair set by the window. Shelves of cloth and leather-bound books lined the walls and stood neatly piled on his desk. He continued to write letters to friends using quills and to answer the increasing quantities of letters that arrived from different parts of the globe. He weighed his letters before affixing stamps and sending them to the post office.

From time to time he posed for photographs, an art still in its infancy. He enthusiastically collected framed photographs of his friends and hung them in his private chapel in his small study. He also sat for some official portraits in the watered-silk robes worn only for formal occasions. In everyday attire he wore his black cassock buttoned across his chest and a scarlet skull cap on his head. Despite his honour, he was always called 'the father'. Leaning on a cane, he remained a familiar and venerated figure as he walked slowly around the Oratory and school. Despite failing hearing, he continued to spend hours in the confessional and generally was ready to receive visitors. Newman himself wished for nothing but to continue his old ways, tutoring the boys in the annual play. He had long ceased to play the viola, his fingers stiffened by arthritis.

In his correspondence he mourned the deaths of the few close friends who had survived with him into extreme old age. Occasionally he noted his own failing health and asked his correspondents to forgive his crabbed writing. A bad fall had left him stooped over and he lamented the fact that he could only read with any comfort in daylight. He had a series of dental problems, requiring the extraction of most of his teeth, and he became ever frailer. While he suffered physical ailments, mostly induced by age, his mental faculties remained alert.

When Andrew Martin Fairbairn, a Congregationalist minister, and soon to be the first principal of Mansfield College, Oxford, wrote four short works on Catholicism in May 1885, Newman responded in his usual manner the following October. He set out his views on religion and reason, arguing for the strong links between the two. Given his advanced age, the response was a tribute to his intellect and to his clarity of expression. It also illustrated his intellectual pride, which had been needled by Fairbairn's criticism. Newman must have reflected, after a lifetime in education and preaching, that the vast majority of Great Britain remained Protestant, with a small, if growing, Catholic population. When Bishop Ullathorne came to see Newman at the end of his life, the old man got to his knees painfully to ask the bishop for a blessing. Ullathorne did not realise how weak Newman was. As the cardinal shuffled to the door to bid farewell to his visitor, he said, 'I have been indoors all my life while you have battled for the Church in the world.'

Cardinal Newman continued to outlive his close friends. Maria Rosina Giberna, a long-standing friend of the Newman family, followed Newman from Evangelicalism to the Catholic faith and was received into the Church in the same year. During the Achilli trial, Maria Rosina helped gather witnesses from Italy and Malta. She later became a Visitation nun and maintained a faithful correspondence until her death in autumn 1885. The old man was deeply saddened and filed her letters in a box marked with a black cross.

After a sermon given on Easter Sunday 1887, the cardinal decided not to preach again as his voice had grown faint. On Christmas Day 1889 he celebrated Mass in the Oratory church for the last time. Nor was he strong enough to celebrate privately in his chapel. When he noticed his hands trembling, he was afraid that he might spill the chalice. His final ecclesiastical function was at a triduum between 18 and 20 July 1889 to celebrate the beatification of Juvenal Ancina, a member of the Roman Oratory. No longer able to walk, he was carried into the church on a chair. Two days later, the cardinal attended the performance of the annual school play, in Latin, which he had arranged, and gave the prizes to the boys.

Two days before John Henry Newman died, he received an especially welcome visitor. Harriet and Thomas Mozley had one child, Grace, who had married Dr William Langford in 1864 and had subsequently emigrated to Australia. In the summer of 1890 she returned to England and, during her vacation, asked to visit her uncle at the Oratory in Birmingham on 9 August. The old man had not seen his niece since she was three, some forty-seven years earlier. Grace later recalled the pleasant meeting. Although her uncle was frail, he held her hand in his throughout their meeting, and recalled pleasant memories of his family. As she left, she knelt to receive his blessing.

The following day Newman felt unwell and, uncharacteristically, remained in bed. He was attended to by his secretary and the doctor was summoned. He entered a coma and throughout the day was silent. The newly consecrated Bishop of Birmingham, Edward Illsley, visited him in the afternoon and prayed the commendation of the dying with the other Oratorians. As evening approached he slipped further, and at twelve minutes to nine, he died quietly in his sleep.

The news of Cardinal Newman's death spread rapidly and tributes poured in. The press was universally positive in his memory and, most poignantly, the bell of St Mary the Virgin, where Newman had been vicar, tolled for an hour when word of his demise reached Oxford.

Cardinal Newman had left careful instructions about his funeral and burial. The ritual of the Requiem Mass was unvarying for every Christian. A field close to Rednall had been blessed several years earlier for use as a cemetery for the community and several Oratorians had been buried there. In a note dated 23 July 1876, Newman wrote, 'I wish, with all my heart, to be buried in Fr Ambrose St John's grave and I give this as my last, imperative will.' Some years later, in February 1881, he added to the note: 'this I confirm and insist on'.

While the practice of burying several people in a grave is commonplace, John Henry's expression of will shows the depth of affection he had for his friend and the loneliness he had experienced since his death. The two, so different in character, complemented each other in temperament. His wishes were honoured.

Eight days after his death, following Requiem Mass celebrated at the Birmingham Oratory, some 15,000 mourners and spectators lined the streets as the funeral cortège made its way to Rednall. The wooden coffin bore a brass plate on which were inscribed in Latin his name, his title as cardinal and his dates in Roman numerals.

The last preparation Cardinal Newman made for death was his choice of a motto for his memorial tablet, which he foresaw would be erected at the Oratory in Birmingham. It reads:

Ioannis Henricus Newman Ex Umbris
Et Imaginibus In Veritatem
*John Henry Newman, from the shadows
and images into the truth*

CHAPTER 12:
SAINT IN THE MAKING

When Newman heard people praise his sanctity he dismissed their pious thoughts. 'I have no wish to be a saint,' he wrote. 'It is a sad thing to say, Saints are not literary men. They do not love the classics. They do not write Tales. It is enough for me to black the saint's shoes.' Yet, two days after his death, an obituary in the *Times* observed, 'whether Rome canonises him or not, he will be canonised in the thoughts of pious people of many creeds in England.'

For many years there appeared little interest in any formal recognition of Newman's sanctity. The Oratorians kept the memory of their venerated founder alive. A dwindling number of friends visited the cemetery at Rednall and Newman was remembered chiefly for his erudition and scholarship.

While Catholics commemorate Newman as the most prominent convert of the nineteenth century, a broader public admired his scholarly writing, chiefly for his views on education. Some of his hymns remained in the repertoire, shared by both Anglicans and Catholics. His poem, 'The Dream of Gerontius', gained a wide public when it was set to music by Sir Edward Elgar in 1900.

Newman's family largely disowned him. His only surviving brother, Francis, who had renounced his Christian faith, wrote an unflattering memoir of his brother.

In his *Apologia*, Newman had portrayed himself as a martyr for the Catholic cause. He did not speak of his abhorrence of Protestant Evangelicalism, nor recount the problems he had with the original Littlemore community, which splintered painfully as some members joined the Catholic Church.

Loyal to friends, easily wounded, nervous and anxious, gentle yet often querulous, diligent in work, a voracious reader, a highly productive writer with a remarkable capacity for concentration, Newman was wont to take on too much and blame others for failure. He evoked devotion from some and approbation from others. His relationship with his siblings passed from amicable to fractious. John Henry Newman was a complex and conflicted character, which is what makes his life so interesting.

In 1945 the centenary of Newman's conversion to Catholicism was observed with a speech by Pope Pius XII. It marked a renewal in interest in the long-forgotten cardinal. The cause for beatification was introduced in 1958 and the process of trawling through Newman's writings as an Anglican and Catholic began. St Pope Paul VI was a great admirer and, in 1991, St Pope John Paul II declared Newman worthy of veneration, the first step on the path to sainthood.

A miracle is required by the Church to vouchsafe the sanctity of a *beatus*. In 2001, an American candidate for the diaconate, Jack Sullivan, claimed that following prayer to the Venerable John Henry Newman, he had been cured of a crippling spinal problem without surgery. The cure appeared to defy medical explanation and several medics confirmed that as the healing had been spontaneous, instantaneous and permanent, the Holy See accepted this as the required miracle for the beatification to proceed.

As the process neared completion, Newman's grave, where he had been buried with Ambrose St John, was opened in order for his body to be interred in the church. Nothing remained of the body and coffin, which had disintegrated since Newman's burial in 1890.

Pope Benedict XVI was a particular admirer of Newman's thought, and in September 2010 he travelled to England to preside over the beatification ceremony held in Birmingham. The recognition allowed for the canonisation process to continue and for this a further miracle was required.

That alleged miracle occurred in 2013 when a Chicago mother of four children, Melissa Villalobos, suffered continuous internal bleeding during pregnancy cause by the placenta being dislodged from the uterine wall. The mother rested as doctors had instructed but the bleeding continued until, one day, fainting from fatigue, she prayed to Blessed John Henry Newman to make the bleeding cease. The haemorrhage stopped immediately. The pregnancy continued over the next six months and the child, Gemma, was born as normal, weighing eight pounds eight ounces. Once more a medical panel was asked to adjudicate the reason for the apparent healing and deemed there was no medical explanation.

This was sufficient for Pope Francis to set 13 October 2019 as the date for John Henry Newman's canonisation in St Peter's Square. Thus St John Henry was declared worthy of universal veneration and his intercession could be called upon by everyone.

EPILOGUE

On one occasion a young man came to visit the house where Newman lived with his small community. Entering the dining room one day, he found Newman alone. The two nodded to each other and the meal proceeded in polite silence.

Some time later in the day, a note was slipped under the door of the visitor's room. Dr Newman apologised in case the young gentleman thought that he had been rude. 'It was simply that I could not think of anything to say.'

The visitor often told this anecdote to general amusement, possibly not seeing the irony that this most voluble man was ever stuck for words. John Henry Newman was an extraordinary communicator and his message arose from a sincere care and concern for other people, especially those who found themselves in pain, isolation or even in despair.

There is something extraordinary in today's world of rapid communications about reading Newman's private letters and public discourses. The image is not of a stainless saint. John Henry Newman bared his soul in his writings and put so much thought and work into the words he used. Few people looked at Newman with a neutral eye; most either were enormously fond of him or strongly disliked him. He could be unfair in his summary of others and often uncharitable. He clashed with Cardinal Henry Manning, a fellow convert and Archbishop of Westminster. Yet Manning's defence and care of the poor of his diocese, most especially of the impoverished Irish migrants, was effective and helped the lives of thousands.

Some criticised Newman as insincere, claiming that he ingratiated himself with the wealthy and influential. Newman might well have seen this as a reasonable observation as much of his focus was on the education of the elite, whom he trusted would in turn care for those who needed to be fostered and protected. He was, after all, a member of a profoundly class-conscious society, whose norms were not above reproach. His means were to educate the mind and convert consciences. But he saw this in terms of combat, in particular against the Anglican

Church. His departure from the Anglican Communion caused an amount of suffering. As a Catholic, he summed up his approach to the education of the laity.

I want a laity, not arrogant, not rash in speech, not disputatious, but men who know their religion, who enter into it, who know just where they stand, who know what they hold and what they do not, who know their creed so well that they can give an account of it, who know so much of history that they can defend it. I want an intelligent, well instructed laity.

With his own words we may take our leave of St John Henry. At the height of success in his professional life as an Anglican academic, he crossed from family and friends to an unknown community, one which would often disappoint and disillusion him. His new life was rarely easy and he often reflected that his decision brought him scorn and insults. As he ended his lengthy and intricate sermon, preached at Littlemore on 25 September 1845, on the task of labour according to the Scriptures, he made his personal farewell.

And, O my brethren, O kind and affectionate hearts, O loving friends, should you know anyone whose lot it has been, by writing or by word of mouth, in some degree to help you thus to act; if he has ever told you about what you knew about yourselves, or what you did not know; has read to you your wants and feelings, and comforted you by the very reading; has made you feel that there was a higher life than this daily one and a brighter one than that you now see; or encouraged you or sobered you, or opened a way to the inquiring, or soothed the perplexed; if what he has said or done, has ever made you take interest in him, and feel well-inclined towards him; remember such a one in time to come, though you hear him not, and pray for him, that in all things he may know God's will, and at all times may be ready to fulfil it.

*John Henry Newman reading a book;
no later than 1890.*

APPENDIX

The Pillar of the Cloud

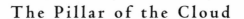

LEAD, Kindly Light, amid the encircling gloom
     Lead Thou me on!
The night is dark, and I am far from home –
     Lead Thou me on!
Keep Thou my feet; I do not ask to see
The distant scene – one step enough for me.

I was not ever thus, nor pray'd that Thou
     Shouldst lead me on.
I loved to choose and see my path, but now
     Lead Thou me on!
I loved the garish day, and, spite of fears,
Pride ruled my will: remember not past years.

So long Thy power hath blest me, sure it still
     Will lead me on,
O'er moor and fen, o'er crag and torrent, till
     The night is gone;
And with the morn those angel faces smile
Which I have loved long since, and lost awhile.

Prayer of Cardinal Newman

MAY the Lord support us all the day long,
Till the shades lengthen and the evening comes,
and the busy world is hushed, and the fever of
   life is over,
and our work is done.
Then in his mercy may he give us a safe lodging,
and holy rest, and peace at the last.
   Amen.